HOMER

ILIAD, BOOK XXI

HOMER

ILIAD, BOOK XXI

WITH INTRODUCTION, NOTES AND VOCABULARY

BY

A. C. PRICE

CAMBRIDGE
AT THE UNIVERSITY PRESS
1968

CAMBRIDGE UNIVERSITY PRESS
Cambridge, New York, Melbourne, Madrid, Cape Town,
Singapore, São Paulo, Delhi, Mexico City

Cambridge University Press
The Edinburgh Building, Cambridge CB2 8RU, UK

Published in the United States of America by Cambridge University Press, New York

www.cambridge.org
Information on this title: www.cambridge.org/9781107621206

First published 1921
Reissued 1968
Re-issued 2013

A catalogue record for this publication is available from the British Library

ISBN 978-1-107-62120-6 Paperback

PREFACE

THIS book is intended not for advanced scholars, but for those who have only read a little Xenophon; and as it is not quite on the ordinary lines, it may be well to explain its plan.

Many years of teaching have convinced me that in education it is not the subjects, but the effects of the study of those subjects on the pupil, which are really important, and that, though for the attainment of certain results the study of the classics is unrivalled, those ends are not generally attained unless attention is focussed on them throughout. In my work a great problem has been how to combine the instruction needed by boys who will some day become classical scholars with teaching that will be of practical utility for those who will never open a Greek book after they leave my form; and this edition will show how I have tried to solve it. What I want is to make the boys think and work for themselves, for I believe that from their own efforts they will gain most, and that the function of a teacher or of the editor of a book like this is to stimulate and guide them, and not to do their work for them. Hence in the Introduction to this book I have tried to set forth the objects at which I think the student ought to aim, to give him hints as to the way in which to work, and to explain the main difficulties he will meet with. Notes for beginners are apt to be too learned, to pass over real stumbling-blocks, and to translate far too much, and mine, I fear, will meet with criticism; but they are at any rate what I have found serviceable for training boys in observation, accuracy, and judgment, and I don't think they will prove as hard as they look. The explanation of most puzzles as to constructions is given in the grammatical sections of the Introduction, and, as I want to force boys to use those sections, the great bulk of the Notes consists of references to and illustrations of points mentioned therein. Of questions of text and scansion little is said—they belong to a later stage—and of translations I have been very chary, for they are precisely the things which the student ought to puzzle out for himself. I don't see, however, that his task need be made too hard, and I know that parents often complain of the cost of a lexicon when a boy is only going to learn Greek for a short time. I have appended, then, a very full Vocabulary, in which much of what would usually be included in the Notes is inserted, and the meanings given are designedly simple so that the pupil may exercise his ingenuity in discovering more appropriate renderings.

My experience has been that, treated in this way, Homer can be read with ease and profit by beginners; that the boys work with more zest when they understand that they are gaining something tangible from their labour; and that even the scientists and mathematicians are glad to have had the training. I shall be curious to learn if other schoolmasters agree with me.

A. C. PRICE.

61 PRESTON DROVE, BRIGHTON.
Jan. 1921.

CONTENTS

INTRODUCTION

§ 1. HISTORY OF THE POEMS.

It is remarkable how little the world knows of some of its greatest writers. Of many of the books of the Bible not even the names of their authors have survived; of the life of Shakespeare hardly anything is told us; and as to Homer, the supposed author of the *Iliad* and the *Odyssey*, the very fact of his existence is a matter of doubt.

Herodotus says that **Homer** lived some 400 years before himself, i.e. *c.* 850 B.C.; but he gives no evidence for his statement, and various dates have been assigned to the poet, ranging roughly from the twelfth to the sixth century: the earliest recorded mention of his name seems to be by a certain Callinus who lived in the earlier part of the seventh century. As to his country too there was great controversy. A well-known epigram runs thus:

ἑπτὰ πόλεις διερίζουσιν περὶ ῥίζαν Ὁμήρου,

Σμύρνα, Ῥόδος, Κολόφων, Σαλαμίν, Ἴος, Ἄργος, Ἀθῆναι,

but at least twenty cities claimed Homer as their own. Simonides—whether the poet of Amorgos or that of Ceos is doubtful—ascribed *Iliad*, VI, 146, to *the man of Chios*, and Thucydides (III, 104) thought that Homer was alluded to in the line

τυφλὸς ἀνήρ, οἰκεῖ δὲ Χίῳ ἐνὶ παιπαλοέσσῃ,

but in this the historian seems to have been mistaken. The idea however that the poet, like Milton, was blind was very prevalent; but it may have been partly due to

the fact that blind men—e.g. Demodocus in the *Odyssey*
—apparently sometimes earned a living as minstrels.
From a tradition that Homer was connected with
Maeonia (i.e. Lydia) comes the name *Maeonides*, applied
to him by some Latin writers.

To the Greeks however of the classical age Homer was
undoubtedly a real person, and so great was his reputa-
tion that, as was the case with some of the Hebrew
prophets, works were assigned to him with which he
certainly had nothing to do. Even as to the *Iliad* and
the *Odyssey* the evidence is very weak. To begin with, it
is most unlikely that we have the poems in their original
form. In the days when they were composed writing, if
known at all, was known probably only to a few, and
men instead of reading books listened to poems recited
at banquets and festivals by the **minstrels** (ἀοιδοί)
attached to the households of great chieftains, or the
professional **rhapsodists**[1], who wandered over the Greek
world. Of the former we have instances in Phemius in
Od. I and Demodocus in *Od.* VIII: of the latter we get a
picture in the *Ion* of Plato. Such recitations, however,
were probably confined to isolated episodes, depending
on the knowledge of the reciter and the circumstances
under which he was reciting, and we are told, though the
statement is of somewhat late date, that at Athens in
the latter part of the sixth century B.C. the Homeric
Poems were collected and arranged at the direction of
Peisistratus, and it was provided that at the great
Panathenaic festival they should be recited in their
proper order. Whether before this they were merely
separate ballads is uncertain, but, in any case, these

[1] " Rhapsodist " seems to be derived from ῥάπτειν + ἀοιδός, because
either (a) they stitched words together in verses, or (b) they recited
hexameters unbroken by stanzas or antistrophes, or (c) they recited
poems the different parts of which were continuous like a piece of
needlework.

INTRODUCTION

arrangements (if true) would have had the effect of fixing the text and making the Poems as a whole familiar to the Greeks, and it was not long before written copies must have been fairly numerous, for "Homer" became a school-book, and we are told by Plato that boys had copies of the Poems, and by Plutarch that Alcibiades chastised a teacher who had no copy in his school. We hear also in Pindar, Plato, and Strabo of persons called **Homeridae**. Who these were we do not know for certain, but Pindar is probably alluding to rhapsodists, and Strabo to some kind of gild of reciters who lived in Chios and claimed kinship with the poet. Plato's Homeridae however seem to have been students engaged in commenting on and editing the Poems. Of such students the most famous were the **Alexandrian critics** of *c.* 270—150 B.C.—Zenodotus, Aristophanes and Aristarchus—to whom the present division into books is due. It was apparently about the close of the Alexandrian period that doubts were first raised as to whether the Poems were the work of only one man; but as to the doubters—the **Chorizontes** (or *separators*) they were called —we know hardly anything, and their influence seems to have been very slight. At any rate it was not till the publication in 1795 of the *Prolegomena ad Homerum* by Prof. F. A. Wolf of Halle (who himself owed much to English and French writers), that the great controversy known as the **Homeric Question** really began. The point at issue was the authorship of the Poems. The traditional view, as we have seen, was that they were the work of one man, and this is still maintained by some scholars and would probably be the opinion of the ordinary reader —as indeed it has been of not a few men of literary eminence—on account of the general consistency of the narrative and its unity of style. But—just as is the case with the Jewish Pentateuch—minute study reveals numerous discrepancies, and this has caused doubt as to whether the old tradition is correct. Critics, for instance, have noticed:

(1) considerable differences between the *Iliad* and the *Odyssey* in language, ideas, customs, facts;

(2) within each of the Poems—and especially in the *Iliad*—many inconsistencies in the narrative, and large portions which seem to have little or nothing to do with the main story;

(3) many passages—phrases, lines, episodes—which appear to be mere repetitions or variations of others;

(4) scattered over the Poems a remarkable combination of alternative forms of inflexion and words borrowed from different dialects;

(5) a certain number of cases in which later ideas have apparently been welded with an older story.

Difficulties have also been raised as to how such long poems could have been composed and transmitted before writing was known, and what could have been the motive for composing them when there were no readers and the *Iliad* alone, as Prof. Gilbert Murray says, would have occupied from 20 to 24 hours of steady declamation.

On the other hand it has been urged that the discrepancies have been exaggerated; that in every great author inconsistencies may be detected; that rhapsodists probably introduced and modified passages to suit the special circumstances of the places at which they were reciting; that writing was probably in use among the Greeks long before the earliest date of which we have evidence; that memories were stronger when books were rare—even in Xenophon's time there were Athenians who knew the Poems by heart; that for a minstrel at a chieftain's court there would have been no difficulty in continuing his narration from night to night; and that if the Poems were not composed by one man the fact of their general consistency is at least as hard to account for as on the other supposition their inconsistencies are. The controversy is still unsettled, but on the whole the theory that the Poems are composite productions—whether as collections of separate lays or as expansions of an original core—seems to have found most favour with modern scholars, and that version of it which is perhaps now most generally accepted may be briefly summarized as follows.

The Poems appear to be European, not Asiatic, in origin, for their sympathy is with the Greeks rather than with the Trojans, and they show much more knowledge of the western than of the eastern coast of the Aegean. Further, they are not the work of a race in a primitive stage but depict an advanced state of civilization. Nor would they appeal to a democratic or commercial community, but seem rather—to quote Dr Leaf's words— "court-poems...composed to be sung in the splendid palaces of a ruling aristocracy." On the other hand the dialect of the Poems is mainly Ionic, mixed however with forms which are thought to be Aeolic, i.e. the language used in N.W. Asia Minor. Hence it is suggested that the origin of the Poems is to be found in lays composed among the Achaeans in Greece and carried by them across the Aegean when they migrated to the northern part of Asia Minor to escape from the Dorian invaders, and it should be noticed that in the Poems the Greeks are usually spoken of as Achaeans and that of the great changes brought about in Greece by the coming of the Dorians no traces are to be found. These lays appear to have been borrowed and adapted by the Ionians, and transmitted orally among the singers and rhapsodists until, possibly in the sixth century, they were committed to writing, and the text was fixed much as we have it now. To the reciters probably many interpolations, great or small, were due; but putting these aside modern scholars think that they can detect distinct stages in the development of the poems. Dr Leaf, for instance, has suggested that the nucleus of the *Iliad* (with which alone we are here concerned) was the Μῆνις, or Wrath of Achilles, comprising perhaps Books I, IX, XVI, XIX (part), XX (part), XXII; that to this there was added by the same or another poet a second stratum including Books II (except the Catalogue), III–VII, 312, much of XIII and perhaps part of XVII, and devoted mainly to glorifying the heroes of the great Achaean families; and that the rest of the *Iliad* may form a third stratum consisting of additions made possibly after the migration into Asia (*c.* 1000 B.C.) and completed *c.* 800 B.C.

§ 2. WHY THE POEMS HAVE BEEN REGARDED SO HIGHLY.

The uncertainty however as to the authorship of the Poems is after all not a matter of prime importance, as the champions of the rival theories themselves admit. "For practical purposes," says Mr Gladstone, "Homer is but one; and his works by common consent are handled as an organic whole," and the doubt as to who wrote the *Iliad* "can in no way," says Dr Leaf, "detract from the magical power which the poem has held over the mind of man from the very earliest days." Let us turn then to the Poems themselves, and see if we can discover in **what their power and charm consist**.

To the ancient Greeks undoubtedly the cause lay partly in their subject-matter. Homer stood to them somewhat in the same relation as the Bible to the Jews. He was, to begin with, the main source of the popular notions as to the gods, depicting them indeed, as Plato complained, not always in an edifying manner, but yet with a remarkable freedom from the grossness in which other authors indulged; and it has been often pointed out that, so far as religious and ethical ideas are concerned, the tone of his writings is distinctly higher than the mythology with which it is linked. "There is no tampering," says Mr Gladstone, "with the greatest moral laws: as far as Homer knows right he works it out loyally into the tissue of his poems.... The cause for which the Trojans fight is a bad cause and receives the defeat which it deserves.... In every single case where he portrays a character radically vicious Homer contrives that it shall be regarded not only with disapproval but with aversion." The Poems thus served also as a kind of text-book of morality. "Homer," says Shelley, "embodied the ideal perfection of his age in human character; nor can we doubt that those who read his verses were awakened to an ambition of becoming like to Achilles, Hector, and Ulysses: the truth and beauty of friendship, patriotism, and persevering devotion to an object, were unveiled to the depths in these immortal creations; the sentiments of the auditors must have been refined and enlarged by a sympathy with such great and lovely impersonations until from admiring they imitated, and from imitation they identified themselves with the objects of their admiration." That this is not mere theory is shown by the fact that Xenophon makes one of the characters in his *Symposium* say that Homer, the prince of poets, had treated of almost all human affairs, and so if anyone wished to become a prudent ruler of his house or an orator or a general, or to resemble Achilles, Ajax, Nestor, or Odysseus, he should study Homer. Moreover in Homer the Greeks found the earliest history of their race. "If you take up the *Iliad* as a record of history," says Prof. Murray, "you will soon put it down as so much mere poetry. But if you read it as fiction you will at every page be pulled up by the feeling that it is not free fiction. The poet does not invent whatever he likes. He believes himself to be dealing with real events and real people, to be recording and explaining things that have value only or primarily because they are supposed to be true." Thucydides referred to him as an authority, and the Athenians in their contest with the Megarians for Salamis appealed to the Poems as evidence for their claim. Further, he was the great national poet, telling as he did of the first great action of united Greece and the earliest triumph of Greeks over Asiatics. "I believe," says Isocrates, "that the poetry of Homer won greater glory because he nobly praised those who warred against the barbarian."

To the modern reader naturally such considerations do not similarly appeal. It does not much matter to us whether the Trojan War really took place as described, or whether, as Prof. Murray suggests, "much of the fighting which Homer locates at Troy...is really a reminiscence of old tribal wars on the mainland of Greece," for to us Homer is not a text-book of theology, of morals, of history, but literature—an aspect of his work to which there is singularly little reference in Greek writers, though, if only from the remarks of Aristotle in his *Poetics*, we can see that there were certainly some who were conscious of his transcendent merits as an author.

Now in literature there are two things to consider—the matter and the manner, i.e. the story and the way in which it is handled. So far as the story is concerned the *Odyssey* has more unity and is certainly more interesting than the *Iliad*, for in the latter the real subject—the Wrath of Achilles—is to a large extent obscured by the number of extraneous incidents and digressions, and Achilles himself, with his sulks and his savage treatment of his vanquished foe, is not altogether an ideal hero. Of course, if the theory of the gradual expansion of the Poems is correct, the original author cannot be held responsible for the later additions to his work, but Prof. Mackail is perhaps not far wrong when he speaks of the *Iliad* as a second-rate subject made into a first-rate poem by the genius of a great poet. When however we try to discover in what this genius consists we soon find we are asking a question to which the answer is bound to be imperfect. Genius is a gift of nature, not an art that can be acquired or a thing that can be analysed into its component parts. The mind of a great poet differs *toto caelo* from that of an ordinary man, and all that we can do is to call attention to a few superficial but characteristic features in which Homer seems to excel. Mr Gladstone, for instance, sums them up under two heads—the thought in strict proportion to the subject, the language fitted exactly to the thought. Matthew Arnold, going more into detail, lays special stress on four points—the rapidity of movement, the plainness of words and lucidity of style, the simplicity and directness of ideas, the air of dignity that pervades the whole work. Leigh Hunt doubts whether even Shakespeare could have told a story as well as Homer and praises the latter for his "passionate sincerity," his truth in "painting events and circumstances after real life," his skill in seeing "what is proper to be told and what to be kept back, what is permanent, affecting, and essential," his imagination "which brings supernatural things to bear on earthly without confounding them." Sir Richard Jebb emphasizes the skill with which he has traced types of character which have since stood out clearly before the imagination of the world, e.g. Achilles, the embodiment of heroic might, violent in anger as in sorrow, but capable of chivalrous and tender compassion; Odysseus, combining resourceful intelligence with heroic endurance; loving Andromache; loyal Penelope; remorseful sensitive Helen; the maiden Nausicaa; imperious genial Zeus: the main outlines clearly drawn, but details suppressed, and much left to the imagination of the reader. Emerson was struck by his cheerfulness—"Homer," he says, "lies in sunshine." Prof. Murray calls attention to his "vibrating sympathy," his "intensity of imagination" pervading even the ordinary things of life, his language "more gorgeous than Milton's yet as simple and direct as that of Burns," and the way in which he takes us into "a world somehow more splendid than any created by other men." In any case, whatever be the secret of Homer's charm, that charm is perennial. "O lovely and immortal privilege of genius," says Leigh Hunt, "that can stretch its hand out of the wastes of time, thousands of years back, and touch our eyelids with tears"; and this indeed is perhaps the surest proof of the greatness of an author, that his work is never obsolete but is still read and enjoyed centuries after his death.

§ 3. TO APPRECIATE THEM NEEDS CAREFUL STUDY.

In reading then a masterpiece of literature like the *Iliad* our primary object ought to be to realize and appreciate its charm, i.e. to enjoy it. This does not mean however to skim it over carelessly with an eye only to the story or plot: if that were all Lamb's *Tales from Shakespeare* might almost as well be read as the dramas themselves. Of course in an epic poem or a drama the genius of the poet is seen in the actions and incidents which develope and illustrate the story, but it finds at least equal scope in the choice and arrangement of the words and in the thoughts they attempt to express. A great author never writes a sentence without a purpose, never uses a word without intending it to tell, and we cannot thoroughly grasp his greatness—and that includes his charm—until we have got to the bottom of the meaning he desires to convey. This cannot be done without an effort, but the effort is well worth making, for, besides the immediate end in view, the habit thus acquired is invaluable and if once gained is as a rule gained for ever. There are few things for which I have

been more grateful than that I was compelled as a boy
to read two or three plays of Shakespeare minutely with
the much-reviled notes of Mr Aldis Wright. In English,
however, except in the case of difficult authors, the habit
is not easy to acquire, for the apparent familiarity of the
words tempts the pupil to read too fast, and to content
himself with the general drift of a passage without a full
comprehension of its exact meaning, skipping all that
seems hard or dull and going on to what looks more
attractive. Every boy knows what an immense amount
of description of furniture or scenery there seems to be
in a French novel, but he is rarely conscious that there is
quite as much in his English stories, only he does not
read it, whereas in the foreign tongue he cannot see so
easily what to omit; and such is still more the case in
Latin and Greek, in which the very difficulty of the
languages and their remarkable capacity for expressing
different shades of meaning force the student to look
narrowly into every sentence and teach him precision
and taste in the use of words; this indeed is one of the
main arguments for a classical education, and one of the
great objections to the theory that classical authors
might just as well be read in "cribs." Before then we can
appreciate Homer we must be reasonably sure that we
understand him, and this implies a good deal.

§ 4. POINTS TO NOTICE.

First there are the **words** to consider. In ordinary talk
we use words very carelessly—we speak for instance of
mortals or *persons* or *individuals* when we merely mean
men—but a great author is much more accurate in his
language, and we shall be making mistakes if we consider
that ἀνήρ is used in the same sense as ἄνθρωπος or that
ξένος is equivalent to φίλος. Every word has its appropriate meaning, every tense and case its special reason,

every particle its peculiar force, though it must be con-
fessed that we cannot always appreciate these niceties of
usage and not infrequently it is quite impossible to
render them adequately in English. The **order** too of the
words in a sentence is most important. Shift it and the
whole meaning may be changed. The student should
read the passage aloud in Greek and notice on what
word or words the emphasis seems to fall. This will call
his attention also to a third thing—that **sound** is an
important element in the poet's charm. And there is
more in this than is sometimes thought. Not only are
the lines metrical and the words sonorous, but there is
also great variety in the rhythm, and besides this there
is a subtle assonance, or recurrence of similar sounds,
too frequent to be merely accidental. Take, for instance,
the opening lines of this book, and notice the recurrence
of the sound of *o* in lines 1 and 2; how πόρον is taken up
by ποταμοῖο in 1; the repetition of the dentals τ and δ in
2 and 3; the thrice repeated π in 4, followed by the
double initial *a* in Ἀχαιοὶ ἀτυζόμενοι; the τ in five suc-
cessive words in 5, and so on. This "alliteration," as it is
called, is constantly found in poets. It is the regular
mark of Anglo-Saxon verse, and is very conspicuous in
Swinburne, e.g.

> O sweet stray sister, O shifting swallow,
> The heart's division divideth us.
> Thy heart is light as a leaf of a tree.

In Latin it is quite common. It is found also in Hebrew,
though what is noteworthy there is the repetition not so
much of a sound as of an idea or of an emphatic word.
This last can also be seen in Homer, for there is a distinct
tendency when a word, and especially a striking one, has
been used to repeat it again within a few lines, e.g.

41 and 42 ἔδωκεν (both at end of a line).
53 μεγαλήτορα. 55 μεγαλήτορες.

62 ἐρύξει. 63 ἐρύκει (both at end).

65 and 68 μεμαώς.

128 and 133 εἰς ὅ κε.

173 ἐρυσσάμενος. 175 ἐρύσσαι. 176 ἐρύσσεσθαι.

243 and 246 ἐριποῦσα.

255 and 271 ὕπαιθα.

302 and 307 ὑψόσε.

386 ἄητο. 395 ἄητον.

395 ἀνῆκεν. 396 ἀνῆκας (both at end).

471 ἀγροτέρη. 486 ἀγροτέρας.

539 and 548 ἀλάλκοι (both at end).

566 ἀνθρώπων. 569 ἄνθρωποι (both at end).

Sometimes there is a slight variation, e.g.

482 μένος ἀντιφέρεσθαι. 488 μένος ἀντιφερίζεις (both at end).

Sometimes the words are different but resemble one another somewhat in form or sound, e.g.

59 πολιῆς and πολέας.

523 ἀνῆκε. 524 ἐφῆκεν. 525 ἔθηκεν (all at end).

534 ἀλέντες. 536 ἄληται (both at end).

Possibly we may refer to the same tendency the repetition of phrases, so familiar to every reader of Homer, e.g.

ἔπεα πτερόεντα προσηύδα (73, 368, 409, 419; slightly varied in 121, 427).

χειρὶ παχείῃ (175, 403, 424).

ἐρύκακε δῶρα θεοῖο (165; slightly varied in 594).

σμερδαλέον κονάβιζεν (255; slightly varied in 593).

εὐρὺ ῥέων (157, 186, 304).

θεσπιδαὲς πῦρ (342, 381).

λοιγὸν ἀλάλκοι (138, 250, 539).

κῦδος ἀρέσθαι (543, 596).

δαικταμένων αἰζηῶν (146, 301).

κατακτάμεναι μενεαίνων (140, 170; slightly varied in 33).

δῖος Ἀχιλλεύς (39, 49, 67, etc.).

ποδάρκης Ἀχιλλεύς (149, 265; slightly varied in 222).
οὐρανὸν εὐρύν (267, 272, 522).
λευκώλενος Ἥρη (377, 418, 434, 512).
ἑκάεργος Ἀπόλλων (461, 478).

In several of the above references slight variations
have been noted, and these, by suggesting the other
phrase, seem rather to emphasize the repetition; but in
the following passages there appears to be a distinct
attempt to avoid the recurrence of a word.

241 πόδεσσιν. 247 ποσί. 269 ποσσίν. 271 ποδοῖιν.
505 ποτί. 507 προτί. 514 πρός.

The striking change of Ἄλταο (85) to Ἄλτεω (86) is
probably to be accounted for by the second line having
crept into the text at a later date, but these lines will
illustrate also the way in which Homer often links one
line on to its predecessor by the repetition of an emphatic
word or something equivalent to it. Cf. Ἀξιοῦ in 158,
τρίς in 177.

§ 5. HINTS AS TO TRANSLATION.

Such then are some of the points to which we must
attend if we would understand Homer. But it is one
thing to understand an author and quite another to
translate him. I do not believe it is ever possible to convey the full and exact force of one language through the
medium of another. Dickens translated into French and
Shakespeare into German seem hardly the same Dickens
and Shakespeare with whom we are familiar, and the
distinguished scholars to whom we owe our best versions
of the classics would be the first to acknowledge the
imperfections of their work. The fact is that in no two
languages are the words exactly equivalent in meaning,
and the associations which invest them are often quite
different, and—especially in the case of the classical

tongues as compared with English—the turns of expression and the structure of the sentences are entirely dissimilar. How many persons have been misled in the Prayer Book version of the Psalter by the use of such words as *soul, hell, vanity, saints, poor, worship*, etc., to represent very different ideas in the original Hebrew? How in translating Horace can we keep the metaphors in *vitulus, juvenca*, etc., without falling into bathos? How can we render into English the meaning of such a phrase as *esprit de corps*, or of words like *virtus, ἀρετή, καλός, πορφύρεος*, or of the epithets *δῖος*, and *διογενής*, or the subtle influence of the Greek particles or its middle voice? Translation is really a very difficult art, and to attain to even moderate success in it requires considerable knowledge of both tongues and no little refinement in the use of words; and hence it is that in translating the classics we are not only learning Latin and Greek but are training ourselves to use the English language correctly. There is no royal road to perfection and it is only by practice that power can be gained. A good plan is to take a passage of some fifty lines or so and to write out a translation of it with the greatest care so as to bring out the full force of the original in the best possible English, and to revise this at intervals until you are—I will not say satisfied, but—convinced that you can do no more to it. Then, if you can, get some good scholar to criticize it, or compare it with some really good translation, such as that of Messrs Lang, Leaf and Myers. Take care however not to consult the latter till you have completed your own version, for there is danger lest the model be turned into a crutch, and instead of racking his own brains the student be tempted to borrow the words of his "crib." Such books, I believe, ought only to be used when the difficulties are insoluble—and there are not many such cases in Homer—or for correcting your own version when completed, or for getting some

idea of those authors or portions of authors which you
cannot or do not wish to tackle in their original tongue.
What you are aiming at is not only the translation of
Homer, but the improvement of your own powers, and
crib-using is like dram-drinking: it may help for the
moment but it inevitably enfeebles him who has recourse
to it.

As to the style of your translation a few hints may be
of service. The first and most important thing is to be
lucid—to be quite sure that you understand what Homer
wishes to say, and to put it into English in such a way
that your meaning will be absolutely clear to others:
vagueness and obscurity are always a sign of either a
muddled head or deficient power of expression. Lucidity
alone however is not enough: your version should retain
all that it can of the characteristics of the original. The
language of Homer is of an antique type, and his style is
marked by simplicity and dignity. To preserve these
features you cannot do better than model your diction
on that of the Authorized Version of the Bible. It is a
good working rule too to prefer a short word to a long
one and an English (i.e. Anglo-Saxon) word to one
derived from another tongue, e.g. don't use *juvenile* for
boy, *person* for *man*, *virgin* for *maiden*, *narrate* for *tell*,
etc. Remember also not to be too free. You are not re-
writing Homer but translating him, so keep as close to
the original as possible, and do not, unless absolutely
compelled, turn actives into passives and objects into
subjects. On the other hand your English must not be
awkward. The constructions of one language are not
always congenial to another. Greek, for instance, likes
participles, Latin long sentences with subordinate
clauses, often introduced by relative pronouns. English
likes neither, so don't carry such classical constructions
into your version. One of your chief difficulties will be
to bring out the due force of the **particles** with which

Homer abounds. The same particle cannot always be
translated in the same way, and sometimes, especially
when two or three come together, it is impossible to
express them adequately in English, at any rate on paper,
for in reading aloud or recitation their influence might
be shown by a gesture, a look, or a change of tone or
emphasis. Among the particles that give most trouble
are:

ἄρα (ἄρ, ῥά)—apparently connected with root of ἀραρίσκω and so perhaps originally meant *fittingly* or
accordingly. It is often used to indicate a conse-
quence or a reason. N.B. γάρ=γέ+ἄρα.

γέ—calls attention to a word or fact, but does not
intensify the meaning or imply that the fact is true.

δή—originally a temporal particle = *now* (ἤδη = ἤ + δή)
or *at length*, but often seems to do little more than
add emphasis.

ἤ—denotes a strong affirmation. It is often used to
strengthen other words e.g. ἠμέν, ἠδέ, ἤτοι and perhaps
τίη. This must be distinguished from ἠέ (ἤ), which
= (*a*) *than*, after comparatives; (*b*) *either...or*. N.B.
Monro says that when used in the second part of a
disjunctive question it should be written ἦε (ἦ): the
first part, it may be noticed, is sometimes merely
implied.

νύ—a shortened form of νῦν = *now*. It is used as an
affirmative particle rather less emphatic than δή.

οὖν—in Homer does not = *therefore*, but *after all* or *be
this as it may*.

πέρ—is connected with περί which in its adverbial
use = *beyond* or *exceedingly*. Hence it emphasizes
the truth of the word which it qualifies, and as some
opposition seems often to be implied it can sometimes be rendered by *although*.

τέ—besides its ordinary connective use is often employed to mark an assertion as general or indefinite.

τοί—denotes a kind of restricted affirmation and = *at least* or *yet surely*. Whether it was originally the dative of σύ (=*I tell you*) is doubtful.

§ 6. METRE.

One other suggestion I would make. Homer is a poet, and to translate him into prose is to lose the majestic metre which is one of his greatest charms. Try to turn then at least one episode into verse. The result may not be brilliant, but the attempt will teach you better than any amount of reading the difference between poetry and prose; it will train your ear to appreciate rhythm, and it will help you to realize more fully the greatness of your author. There have been many translations of Homer into verse. Here, for instance, is Pope's rendering of the opening lines of this book.

> And now to Xanthus' gliding stream they drove,
> Xanthus, immortal progeny of Jove.
> The river here divides the flowing train,
> Part to the town fly diverse o'er the plain,
> Where late their troops triumphant bore the fight,
> Now chased, and trembling in ignoble flight:
> (These with a gather'd mist Saturnia shrouds,
> And rolls behind the rout a heap of clouds)
> Part plunge into the stream : old Xanthus roars,
> The flashing billows beat the whiten'd shores:
> With cries promiscuous all the banks resound,
> And here, and there, in eddies whirling round,
> The flouncing steeds and shrieking warriors drown'd.
> As the scorch'd locusts from their fields retire,
> While fast behind them runs the blaze of fire;
> Driven from the land before the smoky cloud,
> The clustering legions rush into the flood:
> So plunged in Xanthus by Achilles' force,
> Roars the resounding surge with men and horse.

And here is the far more scholarly version of Lord Derby.

> But when they came to eddying Xanthus' ford,
> Fair-flowing stream, born of immortal Jove,
> Achilles cut in twain the flying host;
> Part driving toward the city, o'er the plain,
> Where on the former day the routed Greeks,
> When Hector raged victorious, fled amain.
> On, terror-struck, they rushed; but Juno spread,
> To baffle their retreat, before their path
> Clouds and thick darkness: half the fugitives
> In the deep river's silvery eddies plunged:
> With clamour loud they fell; the torrent roared;
> The banks around re-echoed; here and there
> They, with the eddies wildly struggling, swam.
> As when, pursued by fire, a hovering swarm
> Of locusts riverward direct their flight,
> And as the insatiate flames advance, they cower
> Amid the waters; so a mingled mass
> Of men and horses, by Achilles driven,
> The deeply-whirling stream of Xanthus choked.

What, however, I would recommend you to do is to copy the poet's own rhythm, that **metre** which, as developed some thousand years later by Vergil, Tennyson called *the stateliest measure ever moulded by the lips of man.* Whence Homer got it we know not, but it was marvellously suited to his subject, for Epic poetry is above all characterized by dignity—dignity of subject, dignity of characters, dignity of language, dignity of scale, dignity of metre—and of all metres the hexameter is perhaps the most dignified. Read, for instance, the two versions given above, and then read the passage in the original Greek, and notice how much more weighty and majestic the lines of Homer sound than those of his translators. But the hexameter is not a metre suitable to all languages. By the Greeks and Romans with their sonorous words and their distinction of syllables according to quantity (i.e. as long and short) it was used with success, notably by Homer and Vergil, but the two great Epic poets of later times, Dante and Milton, found other metres suit them better, and by modern writers the hexameter is rarely used, for Ascham is not far wrong when he says *Carmen Hexametrum doth rather trotte and hoble than runne smoothly in our English tong*. Still even in English there are a few poems in which the metre has been used with some success, and from such those who have had no practice in classical versification may perhaps most easily gain some idea of its nature. Here, for instance, are the opening lines of Longfellow's *Courtship of Miles Standish*:

In the Old | Colony | days, in | Plymouth the | land of the | Pilgrims,
To and | fro in a | room of his | simple and | primitive | dwelling, |
Clad in a | doublet and | hose, and | boots of | Cordovan | leather,
Strode, with a | martial | air, Miles | Standish the | Puritan Captain.

Read these lines aloud, and notice how each one naturally breaks into six parts, where the vertical lines are drawn: these parts are called *feet*. Some of the feet have three syllables and others have two: in the former (called *dactyls*) the stress falls on the first syllable, in the latter (*spondees*) almost equally on both. Notice also that in the first four feet of a line dactyls and spondees may be used indifferently, but the fifth foot must be a dactyl, and the sixth a spondee, and in Greek and Latin, where syllables are distinguished according to "quantity," the scheme would run thus

$$\overset{-\;\cup\;\cup}{-\;-}\;\bigg|\;\overset{-\;\cup\;\cup}{-\;-}\;\bigg|\;\overset{-\;\cup\;\cup}{-\;-}\;\bigg|\;\overset{-\;\cup\;\cup}{-\;-}\;\bigg|\;-\;\cup\;\cup\;\;-\;\veebar$$

[To find out which syllables are long and which are short you should consult the section headed *Prosody* in your grammars.]

It is rare to find a line consisting entirely of spondees— Mr Gladstone says there are only four instances in Homer —or with all the feet except the sixth dactyls. A fair number of lines however—about four per cent. in Homer —have a spondee instead of a dactyl in the fifth foot: in most cases this is when the line ends with a word of four or more syllables. As a general rule Homer may be said to prefer dactyls and Vergil spondees, but both poets avoid monotony, the chief danger of this metre, by skilfully intermixing the two kinds of feet, as well as by bringing sentences to an end at different parts of a line, and especially by what is called *caesura*, i.e. splitting up a foot between two words: in Homer the caesura is very common in the third foot. Compared however with Vergil and Ovid Homer is strikingly free in his treatment of the hexameter. He does not care how many syllables there are in the words that end his lines. He lengthens and shortens syllables to suit his convenience. He crushes two vowels into one if necessary. His practice with regard to *elision* (i.e. the cutting off of a vowel at the end of a word before a vowel at the beginning of the next) seems remarkably lax. Much of this apparent license was probably due to the fact that the Poems were originally intended for recitation, and, as the pronunciation of a word depends greatly on the pleasure of the speaker, spelling does not become rigid till reading and writing become common. Even now people do not agree in the pronunciation of such words as *either*, *illustrated*, *laboratory*, *reminiscence*, and it is not long since *balcony* was pronounced as *balcōny*, *tea* as *tay*, *Satan* as *Sătan*. Moreover at the time when the Poems were composed there seem to have been letters in use which were afterwards dropped. The sound of *y*, for instance, appears originally to have been heard before ὥς and possibly ἵεμαι, and by comparison with corresponding words in Latin—e.g. ἅλς and *sal*, ἕξ and *sex*, ἅλλομαι and *salio*, οἶνος and *vinum*, εἴκοσι and *viginti*—we can detect the loss of σ and ϝ, and this may account for much that seems exceptional in scansion and also in grammar.

§ 7. GRAMMAR.

To the **grammar** of Homer great attention ought to be paid; for, though the primary object of reading the Poems is to enjoy them as literature, the style in which they are written is so different from the Attic Greek to which we are accustomed that they cannot easily be understood unless we grasp first the peculiarities of their language, and this will have the further advantage that, as the *Iliad* and the *Odyssey* are the oldest Greek writings that we possess, we find in them the origin and explanation of many of the forms and constructions used by later authors. It is just the same in English. We read Chaucer primarily as literature, but we can also get from him much that is of the highest interest and value with regard to the history of our language. To say that the two ends are incompatible is absurd, though I fear that both teachers and examiners have been too often to blame for devoting their attention so exclusively to the minutiae of grammar that the literary charm of an author is entirely lost to the pupil. I will only attempt then to call attention here to those points which seem essential for the right comprehension of this book.

Before going into details there are three things which should be carefully borne in mind. (1) The language of the Poems is of course Greek, but it is Greek of a very old type, as far removed from that of Xenophon and Euripides as the language of Chaucer and Wiclif is from the English spoken at the present day. (2) It is in the main the dialect used not in Attica but in the Ionian cities of Asia Minor, intermixed to a certain extent with words and forms taken from other dialects and apparently at different periods. (3) Words and inflexions are treated with the greatest freedom and without the slightest regard for consistency. Augments, for instance, are inserted or omitted at pleasure; alternative forms (such as Κρονίδης and Κρονίων) are used indifferently; the same word is differently inflected in different places though the case or person or mood is the same. What probably however will most strike the reader accustomed only to Attic usage is the strange appearance of many Homeric words to his eye and the liberty which the poet seems to take with the **spelling** thereof.

§ 8.

Consonants, for instance, appear to be doubled at pleasure, e.g. Ἀχιλλεύς (39), but Ἀχιλεύς (116); ἔμμεναι (405), but ἔμεναι (411). This doubling, which was probably in some cases the earlier form of the word and in others was perhaps due to the assimilation of some original consonant, seems to be most common with regard to the letter σ, e.g. ὀπίσσω (30), τόσσα (80, though τόσον in 370), ἔσσεται (92, but ἔσται in 223), μέσσῳ (233), ὅσσον (371), and especially in the dat. plur. of the third Declension, e.g. Λελέγεσσι (86), στήθεσσιν (182), ἄνδρεσσι (285), and in the weak aorist tense, e.g. ἐπέρασσε (40), δάμασσας (90), ἐπέλασσε (93). Other instances of doubling are ἐλλίσσετο (71), περιδδείσασα (328), ἀδδεές (481), ὁππότε (112). Somewhat analogous to this is the use in some words of πτ for π, e.g. πτολίπορθον (550), πτολίεθρον (434), φιλοπτολέμοισι (86), πτολέμοιο (433), πτολεμίξω (463, though πολεμίξειν in 477).

§ 9.

Words with an **aspirate** in Attic are often found without it in Homer, e.g. αὖτις (46, Attic αὖθις), ἄμμες (432= ἡμεῖς).

§ 10.

Vowels are treated even more freely. (a) Sometimes they are dropped, e.g. πάρ for παρά (76), κάδ for κατά (318), ἄμ for ἀνά (258), ἄρ (288) and ῥά (51) for ἄρα. N.B. also κάλλιπες = κατέλιπες (414), ἐπανθέμεναι = ἐπαναθέμεναι (535), ἀλλέξαι = ἀναλέξαι (321), ἀγξηράνη = ἀναξηράνη (347), and ἦλθε (57, but ἤλυθε in 39). (b) Sometimes they are doubled where in Attic we should only find one, e.g. ποδοῖιν (271), ἐπέεσσιν (98), λεχέεσσι (124), ἑέλσαι (295); or (c) shortened where in Attic they would be long, e.g. ἔσαν for ἦσαν (236), νείκεσε for ἐνείκησε (470), ἀργέτα for ἀργῆτα (127); or (d) lengthened into long vowels, e.g. Ἀχιλλῆα (138), ὀχῆας (537), or into diphthongs, e.g. ξεῖνος (42), γούνατ' (52), δουρός (60), εἰλήλουθα (81), οὖρον (405), μοῦνοι (443), οὔρεα (485), πνοιῇ (355), πουλυβοτείρῃ (426), while sometimes the simple and diphthongal forms are both found, e.g. (if the same words) ἀτάρ (41) and αὐτάρ (33), Ὀλύμπον (505) and Οὐλύμπῳ (389); notice also ἴσος (227) and εἴσην (581). (e) On the other hand diphthongs in Attic are in Homer frequently resolved, e.g. εὐκτιμένην (40), ὀξέϊ (37), ὀίω (92), and (f) words are often left uncontracted, e.g. ἡμίσεες (7), μεγακήτεος (22), and (g) when contracted εο often becomes ευ instead of ου, e.g. εἰλεῦντο (8), ὀχλεῦνται (261), μευ (150), σευ (475). (h) The Attic rule as to a pure is not observed, e.g. πολιῆς (59), γαίη (69), ἑτέρῃ (71), and η is frequently found where in Attic we should have a, e.g. νηυσί (135), especially in the dat. plur. of the first Declension, e.g. μυρίκῃσιν (18), σῇσι (94). (i) Notice too the tendency in -αω verbs to assimilate one vowel to another, e.g. ὁράᾳς = ὁράεις (108), ἀντιόωσι = ἀντιάουσι (151), ἀκροκελαινιόων (249), μειδιόωσα (491), κυδιόωντες (519), δηριαάσθων = δηριαέσθων (467), περάαν = περάειν (454).

§ 11.

For most, if not all, of these variations there are of course **reasons**. It is common, for instance, in the Ionian dialect to use uncontracted forms, to prefer η to a, to turn o into ου, ε into ει, εο into ευ. Metrical requirements may be the cause of some. Compensation for the loss of original consonants will explain others, e.g. ξεῖνος = ξενϝος, γούνατ' = γονϝατ', δουρός = δορϝος. Often too the Homeric form

is the original one from which the Attic has developed or
descended, e.g. ποδοῖιν, and probably many of the words
with double consonants. The desire also for ease in pronunciation will account for a good deal, and it is quite
possible too that in Homer's time there was, as now, considerable variation in the way in which many words were
pronounced.

§ 12.

Allowing for these peculiarities of spelling we shall not
find the Declension of words in Homer present much
difficulty. For the pronouns it will be best to consult the
vocabulary, but as to **Nouns and Adjectives** the main
differences from Attic usage, so far as the present book
is concerned, may be stated thus:

> Nomin. Sing. A certain number of masculine nouns of
> the first Declension are found ending in -α, e.g.
> νεφεληγερέτα (499). These have been thought to be
> Aeolic.
>
> Genit. Sing. of masculine nouns in the first Declension
> ends in -αο, or less commonly -εω, e.g. Μενοιτιάδαο (28),
> ἱκέταο (75), Ἄλταο (85), Ἄλτεω (86). In the second De-
> clension, in addition to the ending -ου, e.g. ποταμοῦ (52),
> we find very often -οιο, e.g. ποταμοῖο (27), and occasion-
> ally -οο, e.g. Ἰλίοο (probably the right reading in 104).
> The suffix -θεν is sometimes used to form the genitive
> of personal pronouns, e.g. σέθεν (331) and with nouns
> and pronouns following the prepositions ἀπό and ἐκ,
> e.g. ἀπ᾽ οὐρανόθεν (199), ἐξ ἐμέθεν (217), ἐξ ἀλόθεν (335).
> In 295 Ἰλιόφι and in 367 βίηφι have been regarded as
> genitives but as to this there is doubt.
>
> Dat. Plur. of the first Declension usually ends in -ῃσι,
> e.g. μυρίκῃσιν (18), σῇσι (94); in the third Declension
> often in -εσσι or -εεσσι, e.g. ἐπέεσσιν (98), Τρώεσσι (138).
> Genit. and Dat. Dual end in -οιιν, e.g. ποδοῖιν (271).

There are also relics of an old Instrumental case ending in -φι, e.g. γενεῆφι (439), κρατερῆφι βίηφιν (501), and τῶ (432) and ἁμαρτῆ (162) have also been regarded as Instrumentals.

The compensation for lost consonants is not always the same as in Attic: thus we find Ἀχιλλῆος (15) as genitive and Ἀχιλλῆα (550) as accusative of Ἀχιλλεύς, ὀχῆας (537) as accusative plur. of ὀχεύς, πόληος (516) of πόλις, though πόλιος also is found in 540: in Πηλέος (139) compensation is entirely omitted.

Some seeming eccentricities of declension are due to the existence of double stems, e.g. γούνατα (52) but γοῦνα (611), ἀνέρι (213) but ἀνδρῶν (215); πολέες (586) and πολέας (59) come from πολύς, but πολλόν (107) from πολλός.

§ 13.

In **Verbs** the differences are more marked. Take, for instance, the **tenses**. (*a*) One there is quite unknown in Attic—a past, though unaugmented, tense ending in -σκον, e.g. φορέεσκον (31), βουκολέεσκες (448): it is said to denote repeated action, but the iterative sense is not always easy to detect. (*b*) Then there is a strangely formed aorist with the stem of the weak aorist but the endings of the strong, e.g. ἷξον (1), ὄρσεο (331), ἐδύσετο (515). (*c*) Strong aorists of unfamiliar appearance are very common: thus from ὄρνυμι we find ὦρτο (248), ὄρμενον (14); from πίμπλημι πλῆτο (16), ἔμπλητο (607); from λύω λύμην (80, 114); from χέω χύντο (181, 610), ἐκχυμένοιο (300); from σεύω σύτο (167, 227, 423); from ἄλλομαι ἆλτο (174, 140); from ἐρείπω ἐριποῦσα (243); from βάλλω βλημένου (594), ξυμβλήμεναι (578). (*d*) Reduplicated aorists also are common, e.g. ἔπεφνον (55), πεφιδέσθαι (101), ἀλάλκοι (138), κέκλετ᾽ (307), ἐρύκακε (165) or ἠρύκακε (594), μέμβλετο (516) and perhaps προσέειπε (149). Notice too (*e*) the queer aorist ἀποέργαθε (599), and (*f*) the perfects πεφυζότες (6), πε-

πτεῶτ' (503), κεκοτηότι (456), ἔοργας (399), ἔολπας (583), δείδια
(536) and δείδοικε (198), μεμαώς (65) and μέμονας (481), and
(g) the common doubling of σ in such words as ἐπέρασσε
(40), δάμασσας (90), ἐπέλασσε (93). (h) The augment is
about as often omitted as inserted, and (i) words are
contracted or left uncontracted at pleasure: the contraction of εο into ευ has been already noticed.

§ 14.

Look next at the **person-endings**. In this book we
find the following unfamiliar forms:

2nd Sing.   εἶς (150), pres. ind. of εἰμί: perhaps=ἔσσι.
        ἐθέλησθα (484), pres. subj. act. of ἐθέλω.
        ἐμπίπληθι (311), pres. imp. act. of ἐμπίπλημι:
          though ἴστη in 313.
        εἰρύσαο (230), aor. ind. mid. of ἐρύω.
        ὀλοφύρεαι (106), pres. ind. mid. of ὀλοφύρομαι.
        Cf. εἴσεαι (292), fut. ind. mid. of οἶδα.
           πίθηαι (293), aor. subj. mid. of πείθω.
           μέμνηαι (442), perf. ind. mid. of μιμ-
             νήσκω.
3rd Sing.   λάβῃσιν (24) aor. subj. act. of λαμβάνω.
        Cf. βάλῃσι (104) from βάλλω.
           φάγῃσι (127) from ἐσθίω.
           φύγῃσι (296) from φεύγω.
1st Plur.   γενόμεσθα (89), aor. ind. mid. of γίγνομαι.
3rd Plur.   πεφοβήατο (206), plup. ind. pass. of φοβέω.
        Cf. μαχοίατο (429), pres. opt. mid. of μάχομαι.
        ἔτλαν (608), aor. ind. act. of τλάω.

§ 15.

As to the **moods** the subjunctive and infinitive call for
special notice. (a) In Attic the **subjunctive** is characterized by the use of the long vowels ω, η, but in Homer o, ε,
are often used, e.g. τίσετε (134), δαμάσσεται (226), παύσομεν

(314), φθέγξομ' (341), ἴομεν (438). Notice also the aorists δαείω (61) and κιχείομεν (128) from ἐδάην and ἐκίχην. (b) The **infinitive** active often ends in -μεν or -εμεν, -μεναι or -εμεναι, e.g. ἴμεν (297)=ἰέναι, ἔμεναι (411) and ἔμμεναι (186)=εἶναι, ἐρυκέμεν (7) = ἐρύκειν, ἄμεναι (70) = ἄειν, δαμήμεναι (291) = δαμῆναι, ἐπανθέμεναι (535) = ἐπαναθεῖναι, φευγέμεναι (13) = φεύγειν.

§ 16.

In **Syntax** the points most worthy of notice, so far as this book is concerned, are these.

(1) ὁ, ἡ, τό in Homer is not the definite article but a demonstrative pronoun; i.e. it does not mean *the*, but *this* or *that*. In some passages, it is true, it seems to have very nearly its later force but many of these cases can be explained by apposition and in almost all the demonstrative sense can usually be traced, e.g.

5. ἤματι τῷ προτέρῳ (*on that former day*).
17. ὁ διογενής (*that man—child of the gods*).
71, 72. τῇ ἑτέρῃ...τῇ δ' ἑτέρῃ (*with that one hand...and with that other...*); cf. 166.
177. τὸ τέτρατον (*that fourth time*).
207. τὸν ἄριστον (*that most brave man*).
262. τὸν ἄγοντα (*that man as he guides*).
300. τὸ δὲ πᾶν (*this—all of it...*).
305. τὸ ὃν μένος (*that his might*).
317. τὰ τεύχεα καλά (*those his glorious weapons*).
371. οἱ ἄλλοι (*those others*); cf. 518, 554.
412. τῆς μητρός (*her, thy mother*).
421. ἡ κυνάμυια (*she, the shameless one*).
496. ἡ δακρυόεσσα (*she weeping*).
526. ὁ γέρων (*he the aged...*).

From these instances we can see how the demonstrative use gradually passes into that of a personal pronoun (cf. also 67 ὁ μὲν...δῖος Ἀχιλλεύς=*he, the goodly Achilles*; 189, ὁ δ' ἄρ' Αἰακός=*and he—Aeacus*) and into that of the later

article. It also, like the English *that*, glides into the sense
of a relative pronoun in such passages as:

30. ἱμᾶσιν τοὺς αὐτοὶ φορέεσκον (literally, *straps—these
    they themselves wore*).
35. Λυκάονι τόν ῥά ποτ᾽ αὐτὸς ἦγε (*Lycaon—him he himself
    once led off*).

Cf. also 59, 147, 317, 352, 405, 457, and the use of ὅ περ
in 107. In fact ὅς itself was probably originally a demonstrative—at any rate it certainly has a demonstrative
sense in 198 ἀλλὰ καὶ ὃς δείδοικε and in the colloquialism ἦ
δ᾽ ὅς so common in Plato—and so phrases like ὃν...τέκετο
Ζεύς (2) would have meant at first *this man Zeus begat*.

§ 17.

(2) As to the **concords** notice that duals are constantly
put in agreement with plurals, e.g.

115. χεῖρε...ἀμφοτέρας.
285. στήτην...λαβόντες.
426. τὼ μὲν ἄρ᾽ ἄμφω κείντο.

and that neuter plurals may, e.g. γοῦνα σαῶσαι (611), but
need not have verbs in the singular, e.g. τεύχεα...πλῶον
(301).

§ 18.

(3) In the syntax of **verbs** there are several things to
notice, viz. (*a*) the frequent use of the imperfect tense
where we might have expected an aorist, and of the
middle voice instead of the active, e.g. τέκετο (2), ὁρῶμαι
(54), φάτο (114): on the other hand in ὀίω (92) we have
an active form where in Attic a middle would be used.
(*b*) The common use of the infinitive in an explanatory or
final sense e.g. φευγέμεναι (13), κατάγειν (32), νέεσθαι (48),
φέρεσθαι (120). (*c*) In some places the infinitive is treated
as an imperative, e.g.

296. σὺ δ᾽...ἂψ ἐπὶ νῆας ἴμεν.
341. τότε σχεῖν ἀκάματον πῦρ.

P. H.

501. εὔχεσθαι ἐμὲ νικῆσαι.

535. ἐπανθέμεναι σανίδας and perhaps δαήμεναι in 487.

(*d*) As to ἄν, for which Homer often uses its Aeolic equivalent κε(ν), the ordinary Attic custom is to insert the particle when the subjunctive is used in conditional, temporal, or relative sentences, but Homer sometimes inserts it, e.g. ὅν κε λάβῃσιν (24), but often omits it, especially in general statements, e.g. ὅστις...φύγῃ (103), ὁππότε... ἕληται (112). Cf. also 199, 257, 283, 323, 346, 347, 522, 576. He, also, though not in this book, uses κε(ν), but rarely ἄν, with a future indic., and in a principal sentence often omits ἄν with a potential optative and uses the subjunctive with and without ἄν in a future sense. In 226 κε is used with the subjunctive in apparently an indirect question.

§ 19.

(4) As to the **cases** we are at once struck by the fact that in Homer they are constantly found alone to express meanings for which in later Greek the addition of a preposition would usually be required, and as this explains many constructions in both Greek and Latin it will be well worth while to look more closely into the matter.

Of the **nominative** and **vocative** we need say little for they are used just as in Attic, the former to denote the subject or complement of a sentence or words in apposition to either, the latter the person addressed. It may be noted however that the nominative is sometimes used for the vocative, e.g. ἀλλά, φίλος, θάνε καὶ σύ (106)—and that a word is regularly interposed between a vocative and the connecting particle—e.g. Λητοῖ, ἐγὼ δέ τοι οὔ τι μαχήσομαι (498).

§ 20.

Of the **accusative** the commonest use is (*a*) as the direct object of a verb. Of this there are innumerable instances, e.g. ὅν...τέκετο Ζεύς (2), and from this usage probably came the construction of the accusative and infinitive, e.g. ἤ μ' ἔφατο...ὀλέεσθαι (277) = *who said of me that I should perish*, and such exceptional phrases as ἄπορα πόριμος (Aesch.), καί σε φύξιμος οὐδείς (Soph.), *quid tibi hanc curatio est rem?* (Plaut.), and τίν' ἀεὶ τάκεις οἰμωγὰν 'Αγαμέμνονα; (Soph.) where 'Αγαμέμνονα is governed by the whole phrase (= *why dost thou always lament*). Under the same head too we may perhaps class the accusative of the object to which motion is directed, very common after compound verbs and after ἵκω, ἱκάνω and ἱκνέομαι, e.g. πόρον ἷξον (1), Λῆμνον ἐπέρασσε (40), ἵκετο δῶμα (44), "Ολυμπον ἵκανε (505). This accusative is often found in Greek and Latin poetry and also in Latin prose with names of towns, etc., and in such phrases as *infitias iri, amatum iri*, etc., and it seems to appear in English in such expressions as *to go home, ere we could arrive the point proposed* (Shakesp.), etc.

These accusatives all denote some object external to the verb, but there are besides (*b*) a very large number of passages in which the case is used in what is practically an adverbial sense, to emphasize, define, or modify the action of the verb. The most familiar type of this is that which is known as the cognate accusative, or the accusative of kindred meaning, e.g. *servit servitutem* (= *he serves in a servile manner*), but the noun need not necessarily be of the same root as the verb and may have an adjective in agreement with it, e.g. ὀλέεσθε κακὸν μόρον (133), or instead of the noun and adjective a neuter adjective may be used, a construction exceedingly common in Homer, e.g. μεγάλ' ἴαχον (10), εὐρὺ ῥέοντος (157), μέγα...ὤτρυνεν (299), μέμονεν...ἶσα θεοῖσι (315), πολλὰ λισσόμενος (368), πυκνὰ... στενάχοντα (417), ἡδὺ γελάσσας (508), μέγα κυδιόωντες (519), σμερδαλέον κονάβησε (593): extensions of the same use are seen in such phrases as τάκεις οἰμωγάν (Soph.), ἕλκος τυφλωθέν (Soph.), *vox hominem sonat* (Verg.), *saltare Cyclopa* (Hor.), etc. Under the adverbial accusative too fall such uses as γένος ἔμμεναι (186, "respect"), δέμας δ' ἄνδρεσσιν εἴκτην (285, "part affected"), ἔνδεκα δ' ἤματα... ἐτέρπετο (45, "duration"), ὕδατι ῥόον ἡγεμονεύῃ (258), and perhaps τυτθὸν ὑπεκπροθέοντα (604, "space"), and the numerous instances of τι (=somewhat) and τί, τίη or τίπτε (=why), e.g. εἰ δύναταί τι χραισμεῖν (192), μήτ' ἄρ τι λίην τρέε μήτε τι τάρβει (288), τίη ὀλοφύρεαι οὕτως; (106), τίπτε...θεοὺς... ξυνελαύνεις; (394), and such uses of the relative (originally= in respect of which) as ὅ μευ ἔτλης ἀντίος ἐλθεῖν (150), ὅ τοι μάλα πόλλ' ἐπέτελλε (230), ὅτι μοι μένος ἰσοφαρίζεις (411).

(c) Sometimes we find **two accusatives with a verb**. Homer, for instance, is very fond of using what is called the accusative of the whole and the part, e.g. ὁ δ' ἐρινεὸν... τάμνε νέους ὄρπηκας (37), τῷ δ' ἑτέρῳ μιν πῆχυν...βάλε (166), γαστέρα γάρ μιν τύψε (180), τὸν δὲ σκότος ὄσσε κάλυψεν (181), while in 122 we get three accusatives—οἵ σ' ὠτειλὴν αἷμ' ἀπολιχμήσονται. In such passages the "whole" may be regarded as the direct object and the "part" as adverbial, and the same explanation may perhaps apply to such constructions as Ἀθηναίην ἔπεα πτερόεντα προσηύδα (419) and τίς νύ σε τοιάδ' ἔρεξε; (509).

§ 21.

(a) If the accusative is pre-eminently the case of the direct object, to the **dative** may certainly be assigned the province of the remoter object, i.e. its special function is to denote the person to or for whom something is done and whose interests for weal or woe are involved in the action of the verb. It is used thus with great freedom and sometimes the allusion is so subtle that it is difficult to say with precision under what head—advantage, recipient, possessor, ethic, etc.—the instance in question ought to be ranked. The following passages, taken somewhat at random, may illustrate this.

32. δῶκε δ' ἑταίροισιν (to his friends—Recipient).

570. οἱ (to him—Recipient, or for him—Advantage)... Ζεὺς κῦδος ὀπάζει.

307. Σιμόεντι (*to Simois*—Person addressed) δὲ κέκλετο.

39. τῷ (*for him*—Disadvantage) δ' ἄρ' ἀνώιστον κακὸν ἤλυθε.

64. οἱ (*for him*—Advantage?) σχεδὸν ἦλθε.

117. πᾶν δέ οἱ (*for him*—Disadvantage) εἴσω δῦ ξίφος.

138. Τρώεσσι (*for the Trojans*—Advantage) δὲ λοιγὸν ἀλάλκοι.

284. τῷ (*for him*—Advantage) δὲ μάλ' ὦκα...στήτην.

296. Ἕκτορι (*for Hector*—Disadvantage) θυμὸν ἀπούρας.

99. μή μοι(*to me*—Person addressed, or *I prithee*—Ethic) ἄποινα πιφαύσκεο.

218. πλήθει γὰρ δή μοι (*for me*—Disadvantage, or *my*— Possessor) νεκύων...ῥέεθρα.

328. περιδδείσασ' Ἀχιλῆι (Advantage).

414. Τρωσὶν (Advantage)...ἀμύνεις.

130. ὑμῖν (Advantage)...ἀρκέσει.

516. μέμβλετο...οἱ (Advantage?).

306. χώετο Πηλείωνι (Disadvantage).

358. σοι (Disadvantage)...μαχοίμην.

443. Λαομέδοντι (Advantage)...θητεύσαμεν.

86. Δελέγεσσι (Advantage, or Locative)...ἀνάσσει.

258. ὕδατι (Advantage)...ἡγεμονεύῃ.

A further complication too is caused by the fact that with the Greek dative the functions of two other cases are combined.

(*b*) One of these we may call the **locative**, though it applies to time as well as to space. This use is quite clear in such phrases as ἥμενος Οὐλύμπῳ (389), χειμῶνι (283), ἤματι τῷ προτέρῳ (5), ἤματι κείνῳ (517), δυωδεκάτῃ (46), and perhaps in ᾗ (4), τῇ (6), ἄλλῃ (557), but in others the dative may possibly be instrumental and so fall under the next head, e.g. θυμῷ ἀνιάζων (270), ἤθελε θυμῷ (65), κακὰ δὲ φρεσὶ μήδετο ἔργα (19), θυμὸν ἐτέρπετο οἷσι φίλοισιν (45), ὁππότε τις καὶ ἐμεῖο Ἄρει ἐκ θυμὸν ἕληται (112), κεκλιμένον μυρίκῃσιν (18), φηγῷ κεκλιμένος (549), νηυσὶν ἄγων (41).

(*c*) Of this other case—the **instrumental**—we have

instances in ἄορι θεινομένων ἐρυθαίνετο δ' αἵματι ὕδωρ (21), δῆσε...χεῖρας...ἱμᾶσι (30), and from it probably comes the dative of the agent retained in Greek prose after passive perfects and borrowed by Latin poets: ἀπεχθέσθαι Διί (83) is possibly an illustration of this. It is often hard however to distinguish between the instrument and the circumstances attendant on an action and so we find the dative used in such phrases as ἦλθον ὁμίλῳ (606), ἐν δ' ἔπεσον μεγάλῳ πατάγῳ (9), οἱ δ' ἀλαλητῷ ἔννεον (10), ἔριδι ξυνιόντας (390), and Monro says that the dative with verbs meaning *to be with, to follow, to join, to agree with, to be like,* etc., with the prepositions σύν and ἅμα‚ and the various pronouns and adjectives meaning *the same, equal, like,* etc., is generally instrumental.

<h2 style="text-align:center">§ 22.</h2>

Of the **genitive**, which often seems practically equivalent to an adjective, the uses are by no means easy to define, but we shall cover a good many of them if we regard it as denoting something of which some other thing (a) consists ("Material"), or (b) is the property ("Possessive") or a part ("Partitive"), or (c) from which it springs ("Origin," "Motion from," and perhaps "Agent"), or (d) within the sphere of which it operates ("Space," "Time," and many of the "Absolute" uses), or (e) at which it aims or over which it seeks to obtain control ("Aim," including attainment and perhaps failure and the use after words of "ruling"). The list however is not exhaustive, and much difficulty is caused by the fact that the Greek genitive seems to include many of the functions of a lost ablative. This book will supply us with instances of different uses of the case, e.g.

Material, especially common with words of fullness,
πλῆτο...ἵππων (16), πλῆθ' ὕδατος (300), χροὸς ἄμεναι (70).

Possessive, πόρον...ποταμοῖο (1), Ξάνθου...ῥόος (15), πατρὸς δ' εἴμ' ἀγαθοῖο (109).

Partitive, τίς πόθεν εἰς ἀνδρῶν; (150), τί μοι ἔριδος καὶ ἀρωγῆς; (360), ἀκωκῆς...γεύσεται (60), and perhaps (though these might fall under "Aim") γούνων ἅψα-σθαι (65), λάβε γούνων (68), and hence ἐλλίσσετο γούνων (71).

Origin, τῆς δὲ δύω γενόμεσθα (89).

Motion from—not often found in Homer after uncompounded verbs unless a preposition is added or the termination -θεν is used—e.g. κρημνοῦ ἀπαίξας (234). Monro however classes under this such phrases as παύσειε πόνοιο (137), λῆγ' ἔριδος (359), μύθων ἦρχε (287), κρείσσων ποταμοῖο (191), τοῦ μέν ῥ' ἀφάμαρτεν (171).

Space, ᾖξεν πεδίοιο (247), πεδίοιο διώκετο (602), and perhaps λοεσσάμενος ποταμοῖο (560) and αὐτοῦ (17). Monro says this genitive is almost confined to certain set phrases:

Absolute, Ζηνὸς ἐπαινήσαντος (290), ἀρξάντων ἑτέρων (437).

Aim, αὐτοῖο τιτύσκετο (582), ὡρμήσατ' Ἀγήνορος (595), ἰθὺς ἐμεῦ ᾦσας (398), and perhaps πειρήσαιτ' Ἀχιλῆος (580), μή σευ...ἀκούσω...εὐχομένου (475), τῶν περ μέμνηαι (441), μισθοῦ χωόμενοι (457), πολέμοιο δαήμεναι (487).

§ 23.

Such then seem to have been some of the main uses of the cases when standing alone, but it was probably soon found that of the simple case the meaning was too bald and hence **prepositions** were introduced to modify it, e.g. the accusative might indeed denote motion to a place, but it was immensely improved by the addition of ἐς or πρός or παρά or ἐπί with their respective shades of meaning. Prepositions then were originally adverbs, not governing but qualifying the meaning of the cases. For this abundant evidence can be gained from Homer. Notice, for instance, that in 505 we have Ὄλυμπον ἵκανε, but in 518 πρὸς Ὄλυμπον ἴσαν, and in 40 Λῆμνον...ἐπέρασσε, but in 58 Λῆμνον ἐς ἠγαθέην πεπερημένος; that ὕπαιθα seems a preposition in 255 but an adverb in 493 (cf. πρόσθε in

581 and 587, and ἐν in 569 and 571); that prepositions
have different meanings with different cases, e.g. ὑπό in
12, 26, 277, and παρά in 76 and 173; and that the book is
full of prepositions apparently standing alone and governing nothing. These last are sometimes said to be separated
by tmesis from a verb, and plenty of verbs compounded
with prepositions are certainly found, and there are undoubtedly some genuine instances of tmesis, e.g. in this
book perhaps, ἐς δ᾽ ἐνόησ᾽ Ἀχιλῆα (527)—but in nine cases
out of ten the prepositions seem to be nothing but adverbs
and not to have formed part of the verb at all, e.g. κάματος
δ᾽ ὑπὸ γούνατ᾽ ἐδάμνα (52)=and weariness was overmastering
his limbs beneath him, σὺν δ᾽ ἔπεσον μεγάλῳ πατάγῳ (387)=
and together they fell with great uproar, ἐγὼ δ᾽ ἐπὶ καὶ τόδ᾽
ὀμοῦμαι (373)=and I over and above will swear this also.
Notice too that the "preposition" sometimes follows the
verb, e.g. φυγὼν ὕπο νηλεὲς ἦμαρ (57). So far as origin is concerned, prepositions are probably the relics, though sorely
battered, of other parts of speech—nouns, adjectives, verbs.
That this was the case with many other adverbs is certain.
We have already noticed how the neuter accusative of
an adjective was used to qualify a verb. The origin of
semi-prepositions like causa, gratia, χάριν, is unmistakeable.
Such words as λίην (288), ἐπιστροφάδην (20), ἐπιγράβδην (166),
ἀμβολάδην (364), clam, coram, cum, look like accusatives.
ἀντί, περί, προτί (=πρός), ὑπαί (=ὑπό), παραί (=παρά), διαί
(=διά), have been claimed as locatives, ἁμαρτῆ as instrumental. We find adjectives used adverbially in such phrases
as ἐννύχιος προμολών (37), ἑσπέριος δ᾽ ἂν... ἀπονεοίμην (560),
ὡρμήσατο... δεύτερος (595), ἦλθον... ἀσπάσιωι (607). As adverbs prepositions were used to modify the meanings of
cases, and many of them also the meanings of verbs, and,
though some could be used as adverbs also to the last,
others got so associated with the words to which they
were prefixed that in course of time they could not be used
without a substantive or a verb and the case could not be

employed in its old sense without the addition of a preposition.

The chief prepositions or prepositional-adverbs used in
this book are:

ἅμα = *at the same time*: as a prep. it "governs" the dative.

ἀμφί, probably connected with ἄμφω and so originally =
on both sides, or *all round* and hence metaphorically
about, i.e. *concerning*. It is used with (a) dative,
(b) accusative, when verb denotes motion over
space, e.g. ἀμφ' Ἀχιλῆα (240); (c) genitive—very rare.

ἀμφίς, like ἀμφί. For adverb cf. 162 (= *with both hands*).
Used with (a) genitive = *aside from*; (b) accusative =
ἀμφί, e.g. Ἴλιον ἀμφίς (442); (c) dative = *about* (very
rare).

ἀνά (ἄμ) = *up* or *up through*. Used with (a) dative = *up
on* (rare); (b) genitive (very rare); (c) accusative, e.g.
ἀνὰ θυμόν (137), ἂμ φυτά (258), ἀν' ἰθύν (303).

ἄνευθεν = *apart from*. Used with genitive, e.g. ἄνευθεν...
πατρός (78).

ἄντα = *in face of, against*. Used with genitive (= *a match
for, against*), e.g. ἄντα Ποσειδάωνος (477), ἄντα σέθεν
(331). Cf. μεῦ...ἀντίος (150), ἀντί' ἐμεῖο (481).

ἀντί = *in place of*. Used with genitive, e.g. ἀντὶ...ἱκέταο
(75).

ἀπό = *away from*. Used with genitive, e.g. ἀπὸ κρήνης
(257), ἀπὸ πύργου (529).

ἄτερ = *without*. Used with genitive, e.g. ἄτερ κόρυνθος (50).

διά, perhaps connected with δίς and δύω and so originally = *in twain*, and hence *through, thoroughly*. Used
with (a) accusative, (b) genitive.

εἰς (ἐς) = *into*. Used with accusative, e.g. ἐς ποταμόν (8);
of time *up to, until, for*, e.g. εἰς ἐνιαυτόν (444). εἴσω,
which is the regular form of the adverb, is sometimes
used with an accusative, e.g. εἴσω ἁλὸς εὐρέα κόλπον
(125).

ἐκ (ἐξ) = *out from* and so sometimes denotes an agent as

the source of an action. Used with genitive, e.g. ἐκ
ποταμοῖο (27).

ἐκτός=*outside*. Used with genitive, e.g. τείχεος ἐκτός (608).

ἐν (ἐνί)=*in*. Used with dative, e.g. ἐνὶ φρεσίν (61).

ἐναντίον=*opposite to*. Used with genitive, e.g. θηρητῆρος
ἐναντίον (574). Cf. ἄντα (supra) and κατεναντίον (567).

ἕνεκα=*for the sake of*. Used with genitive, e.g. βροτῶν
ἕνεκα (380).

ἐπί=*upon* in different senses, e.g. *on, after, at, in addition
to, in agreement with*, etc. Used with (a) dative, e.g.
ἐπ' (*on*) ὄχθη (17), ἄλτ' ἐπί (*upon*) οἱ (174), μισθῷ ἔπι
(*on condition of*) ῥητῷ (445), ἐπὶ (*in the case of*) Τρώεσσιν
(374), ἐπ' (*in the case of*) αὐτῇ (585); (b) genitive, e.g.
ἐπὶ (*on*) πύργου (526) (νήσων ἔπι in 454, probably=*to*);
(c) accusative, usually of motion to or over, e.g. ἐπὶ
(*to*) νῆας (32), ἐπὶ (*over*) γαῖαν (158), ἐπ' (*against*) αὐτόν
(248).

ἰθύς=*straight towards*. Used with genitive, e.g. ἰθὺς ἐμεῦ
(398), ἰθὺς πόλιος (540).

κατά=*down*, and hence *all over*. Used with (a) accusative,
often in the vague sense of *in*, e.g. καθ' ὕδωρ(14), κατὰ
μόθον (310); (b) genitive=*down from* or *down on*, e.g.
ἔθηκε κατ' ὄχθης μείλινον ἔγχος (172).

μετά perhaps connected with μέσος and so=*midway*, hence
among, after. Used with (a) dative (=*among*), e.g. μετ'
ἰχθύσιν (122), μετὰ στροφάλιγγι κονίης (503); (b) accusative (=*after, to*), e.g. μετὰ Παίονας (205), μετ' ἀθανάτους
(298); (c) genitive (rare=*with*), e.g. μεθ' ἡμέων (458).

νόσφι=*away from*. Used with genitive, e.g. νόσφιν ἐμεῖο
(135).

παρά=*alongside*. Used with (a) dative=*beside, with*, e.g.
πὰρ...σοι (76), παρὰ πατρί (520); (b) accusative=*to,
along, past*, e.g. παρ' (*by*) αὐχένα (117), παρ' (*along*)
ὄχθας (337); (c) genitive=*from*, e.g. παρὰ μηροῦ (173).

περί=*around and beyond*, and hence *exceedingly*. Used
with (a) dative=*round* or *about*, e.g. περὶ δουρὶ πεπαρ-

μένη (577); (b) accusative of motion or extent, e.g. περὶ δίνας (11), περὶ καλὰ ῥέεθρα (352); (c) genitive=*round* (rare), *beyond, about,* e.g. περὶ δ' αἴσυλα ῥέζεις ἀνδρῶν (214), περὶ πάντων (566). For the adverbial use cf. περὶ δ' ἤθελε θυμῷ (65).

πρό=*forward, in front,* and hence *in defence of, before.* Used with genitive.

προπάροιθε=*in front of.* Used with genitive, e.g. Ἰλίου προπάροιθεν (104).

πρός (προτί, ποτί) denotes attitude or direction towards an object and hence *besides.* Used with (a) dative =*on*; (b) genitive=*in the direction of* and so *from, by,* etc.; (c) accusative=*to, against,* e.g. πρὸς πόλιν (4), εἶπε πρὸς ὃν μεγαλήτορα θυμόν (53).

πρόσθε=*before.* Used with genitive, e.g. πρόσθε ποδῶν (601).

σύν=*together with.* Used with dative.

ὕπαιθα=*under.* Used with genitive, e.g. ὕπαιθα (*from under*) δὲ τοῖο λιασθείς (255).

ὑπέρ, possibly a comparative=*higher,* and hence *over, beyond.* Used with (a) accusative of motion or extent and metaphorically in sense of *in excess of, in violation of*; (b) genitive=*over,* e.g. ὑπὲρ νώτου (69), ὑπὲρ αὐτοῦ (167), and metaphorically *in defence of.*

ὑπό (ὑπαί) according to Monro, originally=*upwards* (and so *resisting* or *responding*), and then *beneath* (and so *moved by*). Used with (a) dative=*under,* e.g. ὑπὸ τείχει (277), χέρσ' ὕπο (208); (b) accusative of motion or extent under, e.g. πτῶσσον ὑπὸ κρημνούς (26); (c) genitive=*under, from under, by,* e.g. ὑπὸ (*under*) γούνατος (591), ὑπὸ (*from under*) ζόφου (56), ὑπ' (*by*) Ἀχιλλῆος (15). N.B. In Homer it is better, if possible, to translate ὑπό with a genitive *from under* rather than *by.*

As to the formation of **compound verbs** by prefixing prepositions little need be said, for where the preposition is separated from the verb it ought probably in most

instances to be regarded as an adverb, and even when a
genuine compound is formed the case used with it seems
often to be entirely unaffected by the addition of the
preposition, e.g. in Τρώεσσιν ἐπέσσυτο (227) the dative is
that of disadvantage; in κατέσσυτο καλὰ ῥέεθρα (382) the
accusative is that of space; in ποταμοῖο...ἐκγεγαῶτι (185)
the genitive is that of origin; in ἔμπλητο ἀλέντων (607)
the genitive is that of material. Instances in fact in which
the turning of the verb into a compound alters the construction, e.g. τὸν...προσέειπε (149), τὸν...προσέφη (222),
are comparatively rare.

Three other things may be noticed before we leave this
subject.

§ 24.

(1) That Homer is rather fond of **piling one preposition on another**, e.g. ἀμφὶ περί (10), προπάροιθεν (104),
διαπρό (164), ὑπεκπροθέοντα (604), ὑπεκπροφυγών (44).

§ 25.

(2) That very often we find **constructions implying rest
where we should expect those denoting motion**, e.g. μιν...
χερσὶν...ἔμβαλεν (46), ἐν χερσὶν ἔθηκεν (83), ὅν κε...ἐμῇσ᾽ ἐν
χερσὶ βάλῃσι (103), ἐν δίνῃσι καθίετε (132), μένος...ἐν φρεσὶ
θῆκε (145), ἐπ᾽ ἀλλήλοισιν ἰόντες (148), ἀλτ᾽ ἐπὶ οἱ (174), ἐνὶ
στήθεσσιν ὀρούσας (182), ἐν σάκει πίπτων (241), τὴν δὲ προτὶ
οἱ εἷλε (507), ἐν μέν οἱ κραδίῃ θάρσος βάλε (547), ἔνθορε μέσσῳ
(233), ἐνθεμένη λεχέεσσι (124). The explanation, however,
of most of such instances will be found in the uses of
the dative mentioned above.

§ 26.

(3) That in the Homeric dialect, as also to some extent
in later Greek, there were certain **endings which could
take the place of the ordinary case-inflexions**, e.g.

-φι with different uses: (a) instrumental, e.g. γενεῆφι
(439), κρατερῆφι βίηφιν (501); (b) ablative, e.g. ἀπὸ

νευρῆφιν (113); (c) locative. In 295 Ἰλιόφι seems to have a genitive meaning, and the same may be the case with βίηφι in 367.

-θεν expresses properly the point from which motion starts, e.g. κεῖθεν (62), and so is often employed after ἐκ and ἀπό, e.g. ἐξ ἀλόθεν (335), ἀπ' οὐρανόθεν (199), ἐξ ἐμέθεν (217). The pronominal forms, however, ἐμέθεν, σέθεν, ἔθεν, are often used as simple ablatives or genitives, e.g. ἄντα σέθεν (331).

-θι = at, e.g. κηρόθι (136), αὐτόθι (201), νειόθι (317). N.B. -ι seems to have been an old locative ending, cf. χαμαί (181), οἴκοι, humi, Romae (=Romai), etc.

The ending -δε is not a substitute for a case but is simply added to accusatives to emphasize the idea of motion to, e.g. πεδίονδε (3), ποταμόνδε (13); θύραζε (29)= θύρασδε.

§ 27. ARCHAEOLOGY.

The Poems however ought to be read not only as literature or as a key to the many problems of classical grammar, but also as our chief evidence with regard to the condition of the Greek world a thousand years or so before the Christian era. It is not so much in the account given of the Trojan War and of the exploits of the different champions, though by the Greeks of a later age it was treated as substantially true, but in the incidental notes and references that the real importance lies, for from these we can form a fairly complete picture of the life of that time, a life singularly modern in many respects and in not a few points remarkably different from that depicted by the great authors on whom the fame of Athens so largely depends. "The Homeric poems," says Jebb, "are the oldest documents of Hellenic life," and by careful study an immense amount of information can be got from them. The field has been pretty thoroughly ransacked by eminent scholars, and the results of their

labours are easily accessible, but I would strongly advise
the reader to take at least one book of Homer and try
to find out from it for himself all he can on such points,
for instance, as the social condition of the people, their
religious and moral ideas, their political institutions,
their knowledge, their houses, furniture, dress, armour,
etc. It will teach him how to collect, compare, and esti-
mate evidence—a lesson of inestimable value; it will
introduce him to fresh and attractive fields of study; and
it will greatly enhance his interest in his author.

§ 28. SIMILES.

A word or two should perhaps be said about the **similes**
in Homer. These are numerous, especially in the *Iliad*,
but they are not as a rule lengthy. They are used "to
relieve the action where it flags" (Gladstone), and "to
introduce something which the poet wants to make
specially impressive by describing something similar but
more familiar which he knows he can make clear" (Jebb).
Hence they embrace a wide range of subjects, sometimes
grand, sometimes homely. The similes in this book are
drawn from a cloud of locusts (12), fish fleeing from a
dolphin (22), a man making an irrigating channel (257),
a swineherd swept away by a torrent (282), wind drying
a plain (346), a bubbling caldron (362), a dove chased by
a hawk (493), the smoke of a burning city (522), a hunted
leopard (573). Sometimes the similes seem thoroughly
appropriate, but at others they appear forced and
unnatural. Prof. Murray suggests that the poet may
have drawn some, as it were ready-made, from a kind of
common stock; but it is possible that the fault may be
in ourselves and our inability to sympathize with the
poet's ideas. In any case the comparison should not be
pressed in all its details, for, as Pope says, "secure of the
main likeness Homer makes no scruple to play with the
circumstances."

§ 29. BOOK XXI.

The subject of **Book XXI** is described in its ancient title—*The Battle near the River*. It links on to the narrative of the previous Books thus. Though Achilles, owing to his wrath with Agamemnon, would not go forth himself to the fray he lent his armour to his friend Patroclus. But Patroclus was slain by Hector (Bk XVI), and the Greeks were driven back in confusion (Bk XVII). Stirred by this, Achilles, getting new armour from Hephaestus (Bk XVIII), came forth again to fight (Bk XIX). Aeneas and Hector he would have slain had it not been for the interposition of Poseidon and Apollo, but many of the Trojans he killed, and drove their forces back to the Xanthus (Bk XX). Bk XXI consists of a short prologue and five episodes, viz.

- (*a*) The Death of Lycaon.
- (*b*) The Death of Asteropaeus.
- (*c*) The Fight with the River.
- (*d*) The Combat of the Gods.
- (*e*) The Fight with Agenor.

The last of these Dr Leaf thinks belonged to the original "Wrath," but the Book as a whole he regards as a late addition to the poem. For the student it is instructive as showing the poet's powers at possibly their best and their worst—the former in the Fight with the River, the latter in the Combat of the Gods.

THE TWENTY-FIRST BOOK
OF THE ILIAD

Ἀλλ' ὅτε δὴ πόρον ἷξον ἐϋρρεῖος ποταμοῖο,
Ξάνθου δινήεντος, ὃν ἀθάνατος τέκετο Ζεύς,
ἔνθα διατμήξας τοὺς μὲν πεδίονδε δίωκε
πρὸς πόλιν, ᾗ περ Ἀχαιοὶ ἀτυζόμενοι φοβέοντο
ἤματι τῷ προτέρῳ, ὅτε μαίνετο φαίδιμος Ἕκτωρ·   5
τῇ ῥ' οἵ γε προχέοντο πεφυζότες, ἠέρα δ' Ἥρη
πίτνα πρόσθε βαθεῖαν ἐρυκέμεν· ἡμίσεες δὲ
ἐς ποταμὸν εἰλεῦντο βαθύρροον ἀργυροδίνην,
ἐν δ' ἔπεσον μεγάλῳ πατάγῳ, βράχε δ' αἰπὰ ῥέεθρα,
ὄχθαι δ' ἀμφὶ περὶ μεγάλ' ἴαχον· οἱ δ' ἀλαλητῷ   10
ἔννεον ἔνθα καὶ ἔνθα, ἑλισσόμενοι περὶ δίνας.
ὡς δ' ὅθ' ὑπὸ ῥιπῆς πυρὸς ἀκρίδες ἠερέθονται
φευγέμεναι ποταμόνδε· τὸ δὲ φλέγει ἀκάματον πῦρ
ὅρμενον ἐξαίφνης, ταὶ δὲ πτώσσουσι καθ' ὕδωρ·
ὡς ὑπ' Ἀχιλλῆος Ξάνθου βαθυδινήεντος   15
πλῆτο ῥόος κελάδων ἐπιμὶξ ἵππων τε καὶ ἀνδρῶν.
    αὐτὰρ ὁ διογενὴς δόρυ μὲν λίπεν αὐτοῦ ἐπ' ὄχθῃ
κεκλιμένον μυρίκῃσιν, ὁ δ' ἔσθορε δαίμονι ἶσος,
φάσγανον οἶον ἔχων, κακὰ δὲ φρεσὶ μήδετο ἔργα,
τύπτε δ' ἐπιστροφάδην· τῶν δὲ στόνος ὤρνυτ' ἀεικὴς
ἄορι θεινομένων, ἐρυθαίνετο δ' αἵματι ὕδωρ.   21
ὡς δ' ὑπὸ δελφῖνος μεγακήτεος ἰχθύες ἄλλοι
φεύγοντες πιμπλᾶσι μυχοὺς λιμένος ἐϋόρμου,

δειδιότες· μάλα γάρ τε κατεσθίει ὅν κε λάβῃσιν·
ὡς Τρῶες ποταμοῖο κατὰ δεινοῖο ῥέεθρα   25
πτῶσσον ὑπὸ κρημνούς. ὁ δ' ἐπεὶ κάμε χεῖρας ἐναίρων,
ζωοὺς ἐκ ποταμοῖο δυώδεκα λέξατο κούρους,
ποινὴν Πατρόκλοιο Μενοιτιάδαο θανόντος.
τοὺς ἐξῆγε θύραζε τεθηπότας ἠΰτε νεβρούς,
δῆσε δ' ὀπίσσω χεῖρας ἐϋτμήτοισιν ἱμᾶσι,   30
τοὺς αὐτοὶ φορέεσκον ἐπὶ στρεπτοῖσι χιτῶσι,
δῶκε δ' ἑταίροισιν κατάγειν κοίλας ἐπὶ νῆας.
αὐτὰρ ὁ ἂψ ἐπόρουσε δαϊζέμεναι μενεαίνων.

ἔνθ' υἱεῖ Πριάμοιο συνήντετο Δαρδανίδαο
ἐκ ποταμοῦ φεύγοντι Λυκάονι, τόν ῥά ποτ' αὐτὸς   35
ἦγε λαβὼν ἐκ πατρὸς ἀλωῆς οὐκ ἐθέλοντα,
ἐννύχιος προμολών· ὁ δ' ἐρινεὸν ὀξέϊ χαλκῷ
τάμνε νέους ὄρπηκας, ἵν' ἅρματος ἄντυγες εἶεν·
τῷ δ' ἄρ' ἀνώϊστον κακὸν ἤλυθε δῖος Ἀχιλλεύς.
καὶ τότε μέν μιν Λῆμνον ἐϋκτιμένην ἐπέρασσε   40
νηυσὶν ἄγων, ἀτὰρ υἱὸς Ἰήσονος ὦνον ἔδωκε·
κεῖθεν δὲ ξεῖνός μιν ἐλύσατο, πολλὰ δ' ἔδωκεν,
Ἴμβριος Ἠετίων, πέμψεν δ' ἐς δῖαν Ἀρίσβην·
ἔνθεν ὑπεκπροφυγὼν πατρώϊον ἵκετο δῶμα.
ἔνδεκα δ' ἤματα θυμὸν ἐτέρπετο οἷσι φίλοισιν   45
ἐλθὼν ἐκ Λήμνοιο· δυωδεκάτῃ δέ μιν αὖτις
χερσὶν Ἀχιλλῆος θεὸς ἔμβαλεν, ὅς μιν ἔμελλε
πέμψειν εἰς Ἀίδαο καὶ οὐκ ἐθέλοντα νέεσθαι.
τὸν δ' ὡς οὖν ἐνόησε ποδάρκης δῖος Ἀχιλλεύς—   49
γυμνόν, ἄτερ κόρυθός τε καὶ ἀσπίδος, οὐδ' ἔχεν ἔγχος,
ἀλλὰ τὰ μέν ῥ' ἀπὸ πάντα χαμαὶ βάλε· τεῖρε γὰρ ἱδρὼς
φεύγοντ' ἐκ ποταμοῦ, κάματος δ' ὑπὸ γούνατ' ἐδάμνα·—
ὀχθήσας δ' ἄρα εἶπε πρὸς ὃν μεγαλήτορα θυμόν·

" ὦ πόποι, ἦ μέγα θαῦμα τόδ' ὀφθαλμοῖσιν ὁρῶμαι·
ἦ μάλα δὴ Τρῶες μεγαλήτορες, οὕς περ ἔπεφνον, 55
αὖτις ἀναστήσονται ὑπὸ ζόφου ἠερόεντος,
οἷον δὴ καὶ ὅδ' ἦλθε φυγὼν ὕπο νηλεὲς ἦμαρ,
Λῆμνον ἐς ἠγαθέην πεπερημένος· οὐδέ μιν ἔσχε
πόντος ἁλὸς πολιῆς, ὁ πολέας ἀέκοντας ἐρύκει.
ἀλλ' ἄγε δὴ καὶ δουρὸς ἀκωκῆς ἡμετέροιο 60
γεύσεται, ὄφρα ἴδωμαι ἐνὶ φρεσὶν ἠδὲ δαείω
ἢ ἄρ' ὁμῶς καὶ κεῖθεν ἐλεύσεται, ἦ μιν ἐρύξει
γῆ φυσίζωος, ἥ τε κατὰ κρατερόν περ ἐρύκει."
    ὣς ὥρμαινε μένων· ὁ δέ οἱ σχεδὸν ἦλθε τεθηπώς,
γούνων ἅψασθαι μεμαώς, περὶ δ' ἤθελε θυμῷ 65
ἐκφυγέειν θάνατόν τε κακὸν καὶ κῆρα μέλαιναν.
ἦ τοι ὁ μὲν δόρυ μακρὸν ἀνέσχετο δῖος Ἀχιλλεὺς
οὐτάμεναι μεμαώς, ὁ δ' ὑπέδραμε καὶ λάβε γούνων
κύψας· ἐγχείη δ' ἄρ' ὑπὲρ νώτου ἐνὶ γαίῃ
ἔστη, ἱεμένη χροὸς ἄμεναι ἀνδρομέοιο. 70
αὐτὰρ ὁ τῇ ἑτέρῃ μὲν ἑλὼν ἐλλίσσετο γούνων,
τῇ δ' ἑτέρῃ ἔχεν ἔγχος ἀκαχμένον οὐδὲ μεθίει·
καί μιν φωνήσας ἔπεα πτερόεντα προσηύδα·
    "γουνόομαί σ',Ἀχιλεῦ· σὺ δέ μ' αἴδεο καί μ' ἐλέησον·
ἀντί τοί εἰμ' ἱκέταο, διοτρεφές, αἰδοίοιο. 75
πὰρ γὰρ σοὶ πρώτῳ πασάμην Δημήτερος ἀκτὴν
ἤματι τῷ, ὅτε μ' εἷλες ἐϋκτιμένῃ ἐν ἀλωῇ,
καί μ' ἐπέρασσας ἄνευθεν ἄγων πατρός τε φίλων τε
Λῆμνον ἐς ἠγαθέην, ἑκατόμβοιον δέ τοι ἦλφον.
νῦν δὲ λύμην τρὶς τόσσα πορών· ἠὼς δέ μοί ἐστιν 80
ἥδε δυωδεκάτη, ὅτ' ἐς Ἴλιον εἰλήλουθα
πολλὰ παθών· νῦν αὖ με τεῆς' ἐν χερσὶν ἔθηκε
μοῖρ' ὀλοή· μέλλω που ἀπεχθέσθαι Διὶ πατρί,

ὅς μέ σοι αὖτις δῶκε· μινυνθάδιον δέ με μήτηρ
γείνατο Λαοθόη, θυγάτηρ Ἄλταο γέροντος,   85
Ἄλτεω, ὃς Λελέγεσσι φιλοπτολέμοισι ἀνάσσει,
Πήδασον αἰπήεσσαν ἔχων ἐπὶ Σατνιόεντι.
τοῦ δ᾽ ἔχε θυγατέρα Πρίαμος, πολλὰς δὲ καὶ ἄλλας·
τῆς δὲ δύω γενόμεσθα, σὺ δ᾽ ἄμφω δειροτομήσεις.
ἦ τοι τὸν πρώτοισι μετὰ πρυλέεσσι δάμασσας,   90
ἀντίθεον Πολύδωρον, ἐπεὶ βάλες ὀξέι δουρί·
νῦν δὲ δὴ ἐνθάδ᾽ ἐμοὶ κακὸν ἔσσεται· οὐ γὰρ ὀίω
σὰς χεῖρας φεύξεσθαι, ἐπεί ῥ᾽ ἐπέλασσέ γε δαίμων.
ἄλλο δέ τοι ἐρέω, σὺ δ᾽ ἐνὶ φρεσὶ βάλλεο σῇσι·
μή με κτεῖν᾽, ἐπεὶ οὐχ ὁμογάστριος Ἕκτορός εἰμι,   95
ὅς τοι ἑταῖρον ἔπεφνεν ἐνηέα τε κρατερόν τε."
ὣς ἄρα μιν Πριάμοιο προσηύδα φαίδιμος υἱὸς
λισσόμενος ἐπέεσσιν, ἀμείλικτον δ᾽ ὄπ᾽ ἄκουσε·
"νήπιε, μή μοι ἄποινα πιφαύσκεο μηδ᾽ ἀγόρευε·
πρὶν μὲν γὰρ Πάτροκλον ἐπισπεῖν αἴσιμον ἦμαρ,   100
τόφρα τί μοι πεφιδέσθαι ἐνὶ φρεσὶ φίλτερον ἦεν
Τρώων; καὶ πολλοὺς ζωοὺς ἕλον ἠδ᾽ ἐπέρασσα·
νῦν δ᾽ οὐκ ἔσθ᾽ ὅστις θάνατον φύγῃ, ὅν κε θεός γε
Ἰλίου προπάροιθεν ἐμῇς᾽ ἐν χερσὶ βάλῃσι,
καὶ πάντων Τρώων, πέρι δ᾽ αὖ Πριάμοιό γε παίδων. 105
ἀλλά, φίλος, θάνε καὶ σύ· τίη ὀλοφύρεαι οὕτως;
κάτθανε καὶ Πάτροκλος, ὅ περ σέο πολλὸν ἀμείνων.
οὐχ ὁράᾳς οἷος καὶ ἐγὼ καλός τε μέγας τε;
πατρὸς δ᾽ εἴμ᾽ ἀγαθοῖο, θεὰ δέ με γείνατο μήτηρ·
ἀλλ᾽ ἔπι τοι καὶ ἐμοὶ θάνατος καὶ μοῖρα κραταιή.   110
ἔσσεται ἢ ἠὼς ἢ δείλη ἢ μέσον ἦμαρ,
ὁππότε τις καὶ ἐμεῖο Ἄρει ἐκ θυμὸν ἕληται,
ἢ ὅ γε δουρὶ βαλὼν ἢ ἀπὸ νευρῆφιν ὀιστῷ."

ὣς φάτο, τοῦ δ᾽ αὐτοῦ λύτο γούνατα καὶ φίλον ἦτορ·
ἔγχος μέν ῥ᾽ ἀφέηκεν, ὁ δ᾽ ἕζετο χεῖρε πετάσσας 115
ἀμφοτέρας. Ἀχιλεὺς δὲ ἐρυσσάμενος ξίφος ὀξὺ
τύψε κατὰ κληῖδα παρ᾽ αὐχένα, πᾶν δέ οἱ εἴσω
δῦ ξίφος ἄμφηκες· ὁ δ᾽ ἄρα πρηνὴς ἐπὶ γαίῃ
κεῖτο ταθείς, ἐκ δ᾽ αἷμα μέλαν ῥέε, δεῦε δὲ γαῖαν.
τὸν δ᾽ Ἀχιλεὺς ποταμόνδε λαβὼν ποδὸς ἧκε φέρεσθαι·
καί οἱ ἐπευχόμενος ἔπεα πτερόεντ᾽ ἀγόρευεν· 121
" ἐνταυθοῖ νῦν κεῖσο μετ᾽ ἰχθύσιν, οἵ σ᾽ ὠτειλὴν
αἷμ᾽ ἀπολιχμήσονται ἀκηδέες· οὐδέ σε μήτηρ
ἐνθεμένη λεχέεσσι γοήσεται, ἀλλὰ Σκάμανδρος
οἴσει δινήεις εἴσω ἁλὸς εὐρέα κόλπον. 125
θρώσκων τις κατὰ κῦμα μέλαιναν φρῖχ᾽ ὑπαΐξει
ἰχθύς, ὅς κε φάγῃσι Λυκάονος ἀργέτα δημόν.
φθείρεσθ᾽, εἰς ὅ κε ἄστυ κιχείομεν Ἰλίου ἱρῆς,
ὑμεῖς μὲν φεύγοντες, ἐγὼ δ᾽ ὄπιθεν κεραΐζων.
οὐδ᾽ ὑμῖν ποταμός περ ἐΰρροος ἀργυροδίνης 130
ἀρκέσει, ᾧ δὴ δηθὰ πολέας ἱερεύετε ταύρους,
ζωοὺς δ᾽ ἐν δίνῃσι καθίετε μώνυχας ἵππους.
ἀλλὰ καὶ ὣς ὀλέεσθε κακὸν μόρον, εἰς ὅ κε πάντες
τίσετε Πατρόκλοιο φόνον καὶ λοιγὸν Ἀχαιῶν,
οὓς ἐπὶ νηυσὶ θοῇσιν ἐπέφνετε νόσφιν ἐμεῖο." 135
ὣς ἄρ᾽ ἔφη, ποταμὸς δὲ χολώσατο κηρόθι μᾶλλον,
ὥρμηνεν δ᾽ ἀνὰ θυμόν, ὅπως παύσειε πόνοιο
δῖον Ἀχιλλῆα, Τρώεσσι δὲ λοιγὸν ἀλάλκοι.
τόφρα δὲ Πηλέος υἱός, ἔχων δολιχόσκιον ἔγχος,
Ἀστεροπαίῳ ἐπᾶλτο κατακτάμεναι μενεαίνων, 140
υἱέϊ Πηλεγόνος· τὸν δ᾽ Ἀξιὸς εὐρυρέεθρος
γείνατο καί Περίβοια, Ἀκεσσαμενοῖο θυγατρῶν
πρεσβυτάτη· τῇ γάρ ῥα μίγη ποταμὸς βαθυδίνης.

τῷ ῥ' Ἀχιλεὺς ἐπόρουσεν, ὁ δ' ἀντίος ἐκ ποταμοῖο
ἔστη ἔχων δύο δοῦρε· μένος δέ οἱ ἐν φρεσὶ θῆκε   145
Ξάνθος, ἐπεὶ κεχόλωτο δαϊκταμένων αἰζηῶν,
τοὺς Ἀχιλεὺς ἐδάϊζε κατὰ ῥόον οὐδ' ἐλέαιρεν.
οἱ δ' ὅτε δὴ σχεδὸν ἦσαν ἐπ' ἀλλήλοισιν ἰόντες,
τὸν πρότερος προσέειπε ποδάρκης δῖος Ἀχιλλεύς·
"τίς πόθεν εἰς ἀνδρῶν, ὅ μευ ἔτλης ἀντίος ἐλθεῖν ;
δυστήνων δέ τε παῖδες ἐμῷ μένει ἀντιόωσι."   151
τὸν δ' αὖ Πηλεγόνος προσεφώνεε φαίδιμος υἱός·
" Πηλεΐδη μεγάθυμε, τίη γενεὴν ἐρεείνεις ;
εἴμ' ἐκ Παιονίης ἐριβώλου, τηλόθ' ἐούσης,
Παίονας ἄνδρας ἄγων δολιχεγχέας· ἥδε δέ μοι νῦν   155
ἠὼς ἑνδεκάτη, ὅτ' ἐς Ἴλιον εἰλήλουθα.
αὐτὰρ ἐμοὶ γενεὴ ἐξ Ἀξιοῦ εὐρὺ ῥέοντος,
Ἀξιοῦ ὃς κάλλιστον ὕδωρ ἐπὶ γαῖαν ἵησιν,
ὃς τέκε Πηλεγόνα κλυτὸν ἔγχεϊ· τὸν δ' ἐμέ φασι
γείνασθαι· νῦν αὖτε μαχώμεθα,φαίδιμ' Ἀχιλλεῦ."   160
ὣς φάτ' ἀπειλήσας, ὁ δ' ἀνέσχετο δῖος Ἀχιλλεὺς
Πηλιάδα μελίην· ὁ δ' ἁμαρτῆ δούρασιν ἀμφὶς
ἥρως Ἀστεροπαῖος, ἐπεὶ περιδέξιος ἦεν·
καί ῥ' ἑτέρῳ μὲν δουρὶ σάκος βάλεν, οὐδὲ διαπρὸ
ῥῆξε σάκος· χρυσὸς γὰρ ἐρύκακε, δῶρα θεοῖο·   165
τῷ δ' ἑτέρῳ μιν πῆχυν ἐπιγράβδην βάλε χειρὸς
δεξιτερῆς, σύτο δ' αἷμα κελαινεφές· ἡ δ' ὑπὲρ αὐτοῦ
γαίῃ ἐνεστήρικτο, λιλαιομένη χροὸς ἆσαι.
δεύτερος αὖτ' Ἀχιλεὺς μελίην ἰθυπτίωνα
Ἀστεροπαίῳ ἐφῆκε κατακτάμεναι μενεαίνων.   170
καὶ τοῦ μέν ῥ' ἀφάμαρτεν, ὁ δ' ὑψηλὴν βάλεν ὄχθην,
μεσσοπαγὲς δ' ἄρ' ἔθηκε κατ' ὄχθης μείλινον ἔγχος.
Πηλεΐδης δ' ἄορ ὀξὺ ἐρυσσάμενος παρὰ μηροῦ

ἆλτ' ἐπί οἱ μεμαώς· ὁ δ' ἄρα μελίην Ἀχιλῆος
οὐ δύνατ' ἐκ κρημνοῖο ἐρύσσαι χειρὶ παχείῃ.   175
τρὶς μέν μιν πελέμιξε ἐρύσσεσθαι μενεαίνων,
τρὶς δὲ μεθῆκε βίης· τὸ δὲ τέτρατον ἤθελε θυμῷ
ἆξαι ἐπιγνάμψας δόρυ μείλινον Αἰακίδαο,
ἀλλὰ πρὶν Ἀχιλεὺς σχεδὸν ἄορι θυμὸν ἀπηύρα.   179
γαστέρα γάρ μιν τύψε παρ' ὀμφαλόν, ἐκ δ' ἄρα πᾶσαι
χύντο χαμαὶ χολάδες· τὸν δὲ σκότος ὄσσε κάλυψεν
ἀσθμαίνοντ'· Ἀχιλεὺς δ' ἄρ' ἐνὶ στήθεσσιν ὀρούσας
τεύχεά τ' ἐξενάριξε καὶ εὐχόμενος ἔπος ηὔδα·
" κεῖσ' οὕτως· χαλεπόν τοι ἐρισθενέος Κρονίωνος
παισὶν ἐριζέμεναι, ποταμοῖό περ ἐκγεγαῶτι.   185
φῆσθα σὺ μὲν ποταμοῦ γένος ἔμμεναι εὐρὺ ῥέοντος,
αὐτὰρ ἐγὼ γενεὴν μεγάλου Διὸς εὔχομαι εἶναι.
τίκτε μ' ἀνὴρ πολλοῖσι ἀνάσσων Μυρμιδόνεσσι,
Πηλεὺς Αἰακίδης· ὁ δ' ἄρ' Αἰακὸς ἐκ Διὸς ἦεν.
τῷ κρείσσων μὲν Ζεὺς ποταμῶν ἁλιμυρηέντων,   190
κρείσσων αὖτε Διὸς γενεὴ ποταμοῖο τέτυκται.
καὶ γὰρ σοὶ ποταμός γε πάρα μέγας, εἰ δύναταί τι
χραισμεῖν· ἀλλ' οὐκ ἔστι Διὶ Κρονίωνι μάχεσθαι,
τῷ οὔτε κρείων Ἀχελώϊος ἰσοφαρίζει,
οὔτε βαθυρρείταο μέγα σθένος Ὠκεανοῖο,   195
ἐξ οὗ περ πάντες ποταμοὶ καὶ πᾶσα θάλασσα
καὶ πᾶσαι κρῆναι καὶ φρείατα μακρὰ νάουσιν·
ἀλλὰ καὶ ὃς δείδοικε Διὸς μεγάλοιο κεραυνὸν
δεινήν τε βροντήν, ὅτ' ἀπ' οὐρανόθεν σμαραγήσῃ."
ἦ ῥα, καὶ ἐκ κρημνοῖο ἐρύσσατο χάλκεον ἔγχος,   200
τὸν δὲ κατ' αὐτόθι λεῖπεν, ἐπεὶ φίλον ἦτορ ἀπηύρα,
κείμενον ἐν ψαμάθοισι, δίαινε δέ μιν μέλαν ὕδωρ.
τὸν μὲν ἄρ' ἐγχέλυές τε καὶ ἰχθύες ἀμφεπένοντο,

δημὸν ἐρεπτόμενοι ἐπινεφρίδιον κείροντες·
αὐτὰρ ὁ βῆ ῥ᾽ ἰέναι μετὰ Παίονας ἱπποκορυστάς, 205
οἵ ῥ᾽ ἔτι πὰρ ποταμὸν πεφοβήατο δινήεντα,
ὡς εἶδον τὸν ἄριστον ἐνὶ κρατερῇ ὑσμίνῃ
χέρσ᾽ ὕπο Πηλείδαο καὶ ἄορι ἶφι δαμέντα.
ἔνθ᾽ ἕλε Θερσίλοχόν τε Μύδωνά τε Ἀστύπυλόν τε
Μνῆσόν τε Θρασίον τε καὶ Αἴνιον ἠδ᾽ Ὀφελέστην· 210
καί νύ κ᾽ ἔτι πλέονας κτάνε Παίονας ὠκὺς Ἀχιλλεύς,
εἰ μὴ χωσάμενος προσέφη ποταμὸς βαθυδίνης,
ἀνέρι εἰσάμενος, βαθέης δ᾽ ἐκ φθέγξατο δίνης·
"ὦ Ἀχιλεῦ, περὶ μὲν κρατέεις, περὶ δ᾽ αἴσυλα ῥέζεις
ἀνδρῶν· αἰεὶ γάρ τοι ἀμύνουσιν θεοὶ αὐτοί. 215
εἴ τοι Τρῶας ἔδωκε Κρόνου παῖς πάντας ὀλέσσαι,
ἐξ ἐμέθεν γ᾽ ἐλάσας πεδίον κάτα μέρμερα ῥέζε·
πλήθεϊ γὰρ δή μοι νεκύων ἐρατεινὰ ῥέεθρα,
οὐδέ τί πη δύναμαι προχέειν ῥόον εἰς ἅλα δῖαν
στεινόμενος νεκύεσσι, σὺ δὲ κτείνεις ἀιδήλως. 220
ἀλλ᾽ ἄγε δὴ καὶ ἔασον· ἄγη μ᾽ ἔχει, ὄρχαμε λαῶν."
τὸν δ᾽ ἀπαμειβόμενος προσέφη πόδας ὠκὺς Ἀχιλλεύς·
"ἔσται ταῦτα, Σκάμανδρε διοτρεφές, ὡς σὺ κελεύεις.
Τρῶας δ᾽ οὐ πρὶν λήξω ὑπερφιάλους ἐναρίζων,
πρὶν ἔλσαι κατὰ ἄστυ καὶ Ἕκτορι πειρηθῆναι 225
ἀντιβίην, ἤ κέν με δαμάσσεται, ἤ κεν ἐγὼ τόν."
ὡς εἰπὼν Τρώεσσιν ἐπέσσυτο, δαίμονι ἶσος.
καὶ τότ᾽ Ἀπόλλωνα προσέφη ποταμὸς βαθυδίνης·
"ὦ πόποι, ἀργυρότοξε, Διὸς τέκος, οὐ σύ γε βουλὰς
εἰρύσαο Κρονίωνος, ὅ τοι μάλα πόλλ᾽ ἐπέτελλε 230
Τρωσὶ παρεστάμεναι καὶ ἀμύνειν, εἰς ὅ κεν ἔλθῃ
δείελος ὀψὲ δύων, σκιάσῃ δ᾽ ἐρίβωλον ἄρουραν."

ἦ, καὶ Ἀχιλλεὺς μὲν δουρὶ κλυτὸς ἔνθορε μέσσῳ
κρημνοῦ ἀπαΐξας· ὁ δ' ἐπέσσυτο οἴδματι θύων,
πάντα δ' ὄρινε ῥέεθρα κυκώμενος, ὦσε δὲ νεκροὺς   235
πολλούς, οἵ ῥα κατ' αὐτὸν ἔσαν ἅλις, οὓς κτάν'
   Ἀχιλλεύς·
τοὺς ἔκβαλλε θύραζε, μεμυκὼς ἠΰτε ταῦρος,
χέρσονδε· ζωοὺς δὲ σάω κατὰ καλὰ ῥέεθρα,
κρύπτων ἐν δίνῃσι βαθείῃσιν μεγάλῃσι.
δεινὸν δ' ἀμφ' Ἀχιλῆα κυκώμενον ἵστατο κῦμα,   240
ὦθει δ' ἐν σάκεϊ πίπτων ῥόος· οὐδὲ πόδεσσιν
εἶχε στηρίξασθαι. ὁ δὲ πτελέην ἕλε χερσὶν
εὐφυέα μεγάλην· ἡ δ' ἐκ ῥιζέων ἐριποῦσα
κρημνὸν ἅπαντα διῶσεν, ἐπέσχε δὲ καλὰ ῥέεθρα
ὄζοισιν πυκινοῖσι, γεφύρωσεν δέ μιν αὐτὸν   245
εἴσω πᾶσ' ἐριποῦσ'· ὁ δ' ἄρ' ἐκ δίνης ἀνορούσας
ἤϊξεν πεδίοιο ποσὶ κραιπνοῖσι πέτεσθαι,
δείσας. οὐδ' ἔτ' ἔληγε θεὸς μέγας, ὦρτο δ' ἐπ' αὐτὸν
ἀκροκελαινιόων, ἵνα μιν παύσειε πόνοιο
δῖον Ἀχιλλῆα, Τρώεσσι δὲ λοιγὸν ἀλάλκοι.   250
Πηλείδης δ' ἀπόρουσεν ὅσον τ' ἐπὶ δουρὸς ἐρωή,
αἰετοῦ οἴματ' ἔχων μέλανος τοῦ θηρητῆρος,
ὅς θ' ἅμα κάρτιστός τε καὶ ὤκιστος πετεηνῶν·
τῷ εἰκὼς ἤϊξεν, ἐπὶ στήθεσσι δὲ χαλκὸς
σμερδαλέον κονάβιζεν· ὕπαιθα δὲ τοῖο λιασθεὶς   255
φεῦγ', ὁ δ' ὄπισθε ῥέων ἕπετο μεγάλῳ ὀρυμαγδῷ.
ὡς δ' ὅτ' ἀνὴρ ὀχετηγὸς ἀπὸ κρήνης μελανύδρου
ἂμ φυτὰ καὶ κήπους ὕδατι ῥόον ἡγεμονεύῃ,
χερσὶ μάκελλαν ἔχων, ἀμάρης ἐξ ἔχματα βάλλων·
τοῦ μέν τε προρέοντος ὑπὸ ψηφῖδες ἅπασαι   260
ὀχλεῦνται· τὸ δέ τ' ὦκα κατειβόμενον κελαρύζει

χώρῳ ἔνι προαλεῖ, φθάνει δέ τε καὶ τὸν ἄγοντα·
ὡς αἰεὶ Ἀχιλῆα κιχήσατο κῦμα ῥόοιο
καὶ λαιψηρὸν ἐόντα· θεοὶ δέ τε φέρτεροι ἀνδρῶν.
ὁσσάκι δ᾽ ὁρμήσειε ποδάρκης δῖος Ἀχιλλεὺς 265
στῆναι ἐναντίβιον, καὶ γνώμεναι εἴ μιν ἅπαντες
ἀθάνατοι φοβέουσι, τοὶ οὐρανὸν εὐρὺν ἔχουσι,
τοσσάκι μιν μέγα κῦμα διιπετέος ποταμοῖο
πλάζ᾽ ὤμους καθύπερθεν· ὁ δ᾽ ὑψόσε ποσσὶν ἐπήδα
θυμῷ ἀνιάζων· ποταμὸς δ᾽ ὑπὸ γούνατ᾽ ἐδάμνα 270
λάβρος ὕπαιθα ῥέων, κονίην δ᾽ ὑπέρεπτε ποδοῖιν.
Πηλεΐδης δ᾽ ᾤμωξε ἰδὼν εἰς οὐρανὸν εὐρύν·
"Ζεῦ πάτερ, ὡς οὔ τίς με θεῶν ἐλεεινὸν ὑπέστη
ἐκ ποταμοῖο σαῶσαι· ἔπειτα δὲ καί τι πάθοιμι.
ἄλλος δ᾽ οὔ τίς μοι τόσον αἴτιος Οὐρανιώνων, 275
ἀλλὰ φίλη μήτηρ, ἥ με ψεύδεσσιν ἔθελγεν·
ἥ μ᾽ ἔφατο Τρώων ὑπὸ τείχεϊ θωρηκτάων
λαιψηροῖσ᾽ ὀλέεσθαι Ἀπόλλωνος βελέεσσιν.
ὥς μ᾽ ὄφελ᾽ Ἕκτωρ κτεῖναι, ὃς ἐνθάδε γ᾽ ἔτραφ᾽
ἄριστος·
τῶ κ᾽ ἀγαθὸς μὲν ἔπεφν᾽, ἀγαθὸν δέ κεν ἐξενάριξε. 280
νῦν δέ με λευγαλέῳ θανάτῳ εἵμαρτο ἀλῶναι
ἐρχθέντ᾽ ἐν μεγάλῳ ποταμῷ, ὡς παῖδα συφορβόν,
ὅν ῥά τ᾽ ἔναυλος ἀποέρσῃ χειμῶνι περῶντα."
ὡς φάτο, τῷ δὲ μάλ᾽ ὦκα Ποσειδάων καὶ Ἀθήνη
στήτην ἐγγὺς ἰόντε, δέμας δ᾽ ἄνδρεσσι ἐΐκτην, 285
χειρὶ δὲ χεῖρα λαβόντες ἐπιστώσαντο ἔπεσσι.
τοῖσι δὲ μύθων ἦρχε Ποσειδάων ἐνοσίχθων·
"Πηλεΐδη, μήτ᾽ ἄρ τι λίην τρέε μήτε τι τάρβει·
τοίω γάρ τοι νῶι θεῶν ἐπιταρρόθω εἰμὲν
Ζηνὸς ἐπαινήσαντος, ἐγὼ καὶ Παλλὰς Ἀθήνη· 290

ὡς οὔ τοι ποταμῷ γε δαμήμεναι αἴσιμόν ἐστιν·
ἀλλ' ὅδε μὲν τάχα λωφήσει, σὺ δὲ εἴσεαι αὐτός·
αὐτάρ τοι πυκινῶς ὑποθησόμεθ', αἴ κε πίθηαι·
μὴ πρὶν παύειν χεῖρας ὁμοίου πτολέμοιο,
πρὶν κατὰ Ἰλιόφι κλυτὰ τείχεα λαὸν ἐέλσαι   295
Τρωικόν, ὅς κε φύγῃσι. σὺ δ' Ἕκτορι θυμὸν ἀπούρας
ἂψ ἐπὶ νῆας ἴμεν· δίδομεν δέ τοι εὖχος ἀρέσθαι."
      τὼ μὲν ἄρ' ὣς εἰπόντε μετ' ἀθανάτους ἀπεβήτην,
αὐτὰρ ὁ βῆ—μέγα γάρ ρα θεῶν ὤτρυνεν ἐφετμή—
ἐς πεδίον· τὸ δὲ πᾶν πλῆθ' ὕδατος ἐκχυμένοιο,   300
πολλὰ δὲ τεύχεα καλὰ δαϊκταμένων αἰζηῶν
πλῶον καὶ νέκυες. τοῦ δ' ὑψόσε γούνατ' ἐπήδα
πρὸς ρόον ἀΐσσοντος ἀν' ἰθύν, οὐδέ μιν ἴσχεν
εὐρὺ ρέων ποταμός· μέγα γὰρ σθένος ἔμβαλ' Ἀθήνη.
οὐδὲ Σκάμανδρος ἔληγε τὸ ὃν μένος, ἀλλ' ἔτι μᾶλλον
χώετο Πηλείωνι, κόρυσσε δὲ κῦμα ρόοιο   306
ὑψόσ' ἀειρόμενος, Σιμόεντι δὲ κέκλετ' ἀΰσας·
      "φίλε κασίγνητε, σθένος ἀνέρος ἀμφότεροί περ
σχῶμεν, ἐπεὶ τάχα ἄστυ μέγα Πριάμοιο ἄνακτος
ἐκπέρσει, Τρῶες δὲ κατὰ μόθον οὐ μενέουσιν.   310
ἀλλ' ἐπάμυνε τάχιστα, καὶ ἐμπίπληθι ρέεθρα
ὕδατος ἐκ πηγέων, πάντας δ' ὀρόθυνον ἐναύλους,
ἵστη δὲ μέγα κῦμα, πολὺν δ' ὀρυμαγδὸν ὄρινε
φιτρῶν καὶ λάων, ἵνα παύσομεν ἄγριον ἄνδρα,
ὃς δὴ νῦν κρατέει, μέμονεν δ' ὅ γε ἶσα θεοῖσι.   315
φημὶ γὰρ οὔτε βίην χραισμησέμεν οὔτε τι εἶδος
οὔτε τὰ τεύχεα καλά, τά που μάλα νειόθι λίμνης
κείσεθ' ὑπ' ἰλύος κεκαλυμμένα· κὰδ δέ μιν αὐτὸν
εἰλύσω ψαμάθοισι, ἅλις χέραδος περιχεύας,
μυρίον, οὐδέ οἱ ὀστέ' ἐπιστήσονται Ἀχαιοὶ   320

ἀλλέξαι· τόσσην οἱ ἄσιν καθύπερθε καλύψω.
αὐτοῦ οἱ καὶ σῆμα τετεύξεται, οὐδέ τί μιν χρεὼ
ἔσται τυμβοχοῆσ᾽, ὅτε μιν θάπτωσιν Ἀχαιοί."
ἦ, καὶ ἐπῶρτ᾽ Ἀχιλῆι κυκώμενος, ὑψόσε θύων,
μορμύρων ἀφρῷ τε καὶ αἵματι καὶ νεκύεσσι.   325
πορφύρεον δ᾽ ἄρα κῦμα διιπετέος ποταμοῖο
ἵστατ᾽ ἀειρόμενον, κατὰ δ᾽ ᾕρεε Πηλείωνα.
Ἥρη δὲ μέγ᾽ ἄυσε περιδδείσασ᾽ Ἀχιλῆι,
μή μιν ἀποέρσειε μέγας ποταμὸς βαθυδίνης.
αὐτίκα δ᾽ Ἥφαιστον προσεφώνεε, ὃν φίλον υἱόν·   330
ἵ ὄρσεο, κυλλοπόδιον, ἐμὸν τέκος· ἄντα σέθεν γὰρ
Ξάνθον δινήεντα μάχῃ ἠίσκομεν εἶναι·
ἀλλ᾽ ἐπάμυνε τάχιστα, πιφαύσκεο δὲ φλόγα πολλήν.
αὐτὰρ ἐγὼ Ζεφύροιο καὶ ἀργεστᾶο Νότοιο
εἴσομαι ἐξ ἁλόθεν χαλεπὴν ὄρσουσα θύελλαν,   335
ἥ κεν ἀπὸ Τρώων κεφαλὰς καὶ τεύχεα κήαι,
φλέγμα κακὸν φορέουσα. σὺ δὲ Ξάνθοιο παρ᾽ ὄχθας
δένδρεα καῖ᾽, ἐν δ᾽ αὐτὸν ἵει πυρί·] μηδέ σε πάμπαν
μειλιχίοισι ἔπεσσιν ἀποτρεπέτω καὶ ἀρειῇ·
μηδὲ πρὶν ἀπόπαυε τεὸν μένος, ἀλλ᾽ ὁπότ᾽ ἂν δὴ   340
φθέγξομ᾽ ἐγὼ ἰάχουσα, τότε σχεῖν ἀκάματον πῦρ."
ὣς ἔφαθ᾽, Ἥφαιστος δὲ τιτύσκετο θεσπιδαὲς πῦρ.
πρῶτα μὲν ἐν πεδίῳ πῦρ δαίετο, καῖε δὲ νεκροὺς
πολλούς, οἵ ῥα κατ᾽ αὐτόθ᾽ ἔσαν ἅλις, οὓς κτάν᾽
          Ἀχιλλεύς.
πᾶν δ᾽ ἐξηράνθη πεδίον, σχέτο δ᾽ ἀγλαὸν ὕδωρ.   345
ὡς δ᾽ ὅτ᾽ ὀπωρινὸς βορέης νεοαρδέ᾽ ἀλωὴν
αἶψ᾽ ἀγξηράνῃ· χαίρει δέ μιν ὅστις ἐθείρῃ·
ὣς ἐξηράνθη πεδίον πᾶν, κὰδ δ᾽ ἄρα νεκροὺς
κῆεν· ὁ δ᾽ ἐς ποταμὸν τρέψε φλόγα παμφανόωσαν.

καίοντο πτελέαι καὶ ἰτέαι ἠδὲ μυρῖκαι, 350
καίετο δὲ λωτός τ᾽ ἠδὲ θρύον ἠδὲ κύπειρον,
τὰ περὶ καλὰ ῥέεθρα ἅλις ποταμοῖο πεφύκει·
τείροντ᾽ ἐγχέλυές τε καὶ ἰχθύες οἱ κατὰ δίνας,
οἳ κατὰ καλὰ ῥέεθρα κυβίστων ἔνθα καὶ ἔνθα
πνοιῇ τειρόμενοι πολυμήτιος Ἡφαίστοιο. 355
καίετο δ᾽ ἲς ποταμοῖο, ἔπος τ᾽ ἔφατ᾽ ἔκ τ᾽ ὀνόμαζεν·

"῾Ήφαιστ᾽, οὔ τις σοί γε θεῶν δύνατ᾽ ἀντιφερίζειν,
οὐδ᾽ ἂν ἐγὼ σοί γ᾽ ὧδε πυρὶ φλεγέθοντι μαχοίμην.
λῆγ᾽ ἔριδος, Τρῶας δὲ καὶ αὐτίκα δῖος Ἀχιλλεὺς
ἄστεος ἐξελάσειε· τί μοι ἔριδος καὶ ἀρωγῆς;" 360
φῆ πυρὶ καιόμενος, ἀνὰ δ᾽ ἔφλυε καλὰ ῥέεθρα.
ὡς δὲ λέβης ζεῖ ἔνδον, ἐπειγόμενος πυρὶ πολλῷ,
κνίσην μελδόμενος ἁπαλοτρεφέος σιάλοιο,
πάντοθεν ἀμβολάδην, ὑπὸ δὲ ξύλα κάγκανα κεῖται,
ὣς τοῦ καλὰ ῥέεθρα πυρὶ φλέγετο, ζέε δ᾽ ὕδωρ· 365
οὐδ᾽ ἔθελε προρέειν, ἀλλ᾽ ἴσχετο· τεῖρε δ᾽ ἀϋτμὴ
Ἡφαίστοιο βίηφι πολύφρονος. αὐτὰρ ὅ γ᾽ ῞Ηρην
πολλὰ λισσόμενος ἔπεα πτερόεντα προσηύδα·

"῞Ηρη, τίπτε σὸς υἱὸς ἐμὸν ῥόον ἔχραε κήδειν
ἐξ ἄλλων; οὐ μέν τοι ἐγὼ τόσον αἴτιός εἰμι, 370
ὅσσον οἱ ἄλλοι πάντες, ὅσοι Τρώεσσιν ἀρωγοί.
ἀλλ᾽ ἦ τοι μὲν ἐγὼν ἀποπαύσομαι, εἰ σὺ κελεύεις,
παυέσθω δὲ καὶ οὗτος. ἐγὼ δ᾽ ἐπὶ καὶ τόδ᾽ ὀμοῦμαι,
μή ποτ᾽ ἐπὶ Τρώεσσιν ἀλεξήσειν κακὸν ἦμαρ,
μηδ᾽ ὁπότ᾽ ἂν Τροίη μαλερῷ πυρὶ πᾶσα δάηται 375
δαιομένη, δαίωσι δ᾽ ἀρήιοι υἷες Ἀχαιῶν."

αὐτὰρ ἐπεὶ τό γ᾽ ἄκουσε θεὰ λευκώλενος ῞Ηρη,
αυτίκ᾽ ἄρ᾽ ῞Ηφαιστον προσεφώνεε, ὃν φίλον υἱόν·
"῞Ηφαιστε, σχέο, τέκνον ἀγακλεές· οὐδὲ ἔοικεν

ἀθάνατον θεὸν ὧδε βροτῶν ἕνεκα στυφελίζειν." 380
ὣς ἔφαθ', Ἥφαιστος δὲ κατέσβεσε θεσπιδαὲς πῦρ,
ἄψορρον δ' ἄρα κῦμα κατέσσυτο καλὰ ῥέεθρα.
αὐτὰρ ἐπεὶ Ξάνθοιο δάμη μένος, οἱ μὲν ἔπειτα
παυσάσθην· Ἥρη γὰρ ἐρύκακε χωομένη περ.
ἐν δ' ἄλλοισι θεοῖσιν ἔρις πέσε βεβριθυῖα 385
ἀργαλέη, δίχα δέ σφιν ἐνὶ φρεσὶ θυμὸς ἄητο·
σὺν δ' ἔπεσον μεγάλῳ πατάγῳ, βράχε δ' εὐρεῖα χθών,
ἀμφὶ δὲ σάλπιγξεν μέγας οὐρανός. ἄϊε δὲ Ζεὺς
ἥμενος Οὐλύμπῳ· ἐγέλασσε δέ οἱ φίλον ἦτορ
γηθοσύνῃ, ὅθ' ὁρᾶτο θεοὺς ἔριδι ξυνιόντας. 390
ἔνθ' οἵ γ' οὐκέτι δηρὸν ἀφέστασαν· ἦρχε γὰρ Ἄρης
ῥινοτόρος, καὶ πρῶτος Ἀθηναίῃ ἐπόρουσε
χάλκεον ἔγχος ἔχων, καὶ ὀνειδεῖον φάτο μῦθον·
"τίπτ' αὖτ', ὦ κυνάμυια, θεοὺς ἔριδι ξυνελαύνεις
θάρσος ἄητον ἔχουσα, μέγας δέ σε θυμὸς ἀνῆκεν; 395
οὐ μέμνῃ, ὅτε Τυδείδην Διομήδε' ἀνῆκας
οὐτάμεναι, αὐτὴ δὲ πανόψιον ἔγχος ἑλοῦσα
ἰθὺς ἐμεῦ ὦσας, διὰ δὲ χρόα καλὸν ἔδαψας;
τῷ σ' αὖ νῦν ὀίω ἀποτισέμεν ὅσσα μ' ἔοργας."
ὣς εἰπὼν οὔτησε κατ' αἰγίδα θυσσανόεσσαν 400
σμερδαλέην, ἣν οὐδὲ Διὸς δάμνησι κεραυνός·
τῇ μιν Ἄρης οὔτησε μιαιφόνος ἔγχεϊ μακρῷ.
ἡ δ' ἀναχασσαμένη λίθον εἵλετο χειρὶ παχείῃ
κείμενον ἐν πεδίῳ μέλανα, τρηχύν τε μέγαν τε, 404
τόν ῥ' ἄνδρες πρότεροι θέσαν ἔμμεναι οὖρον ἀρούρης·
τῷ βάλε θοῦρον Ἄρηα κατ' αὐχένα, λῦσε δὲ γυῖα.
ἑπτὰ δ' ἐπέσχε πέλεθρα πεσών, ἐκόνισε δὲ χαίτας,
τεύχεα δ' ἀμφαράβησε· γέλασσε δὲ Παλλὰς Ἀθήνη,
καί οἱ ἐπευχομένη ἔπεα πτερόεντα προσηύδα·

"νηπύτι᾽, οὐδέ νύ πώ περ ἐπεφράσω ὅσσον ἀρείων
εὔχομ᾽ ἐγὼν ἔμεναι, ὅτι μοι μένος ἰσοφαρίζεις. 411
οὕτω κεν τῆς μητρὸς ἐρινύας ἐξαποτίνοις,
ἥ τοι χωομένη κακὰ μήδεται, οὕνεκ᾽ Ἀχαιοὺς
κάλλιπες, αὐτὰρ Τρωσὶν ὑπερφιάλοισιν ἀμύνεις."
ὣς ἄρα φωνήσασα πάλιν τρέπεν ὄσσε φαεινώ. 415
τὸν δ᾽ ἄγε χειρὸς ἑλοῦσα Διὸς θυγάτηρ Ἀφροδίτη
πυκνὰ μάλα στενάχοντα· μόγις δ᾽ ἐσαγείρετο θυμόν.
τὴν δ᾽ ὡς οὖν ἐνόησε θεὰ λευκώλενος Ἥρη,
αὐτίκ᾽ Ἀθηναίην ἔπεα πτερόεντα προσηύδα·
"ὢ πόποι, αἰγιόχοιο Διὸς τέκος, ἀτρυτώνη, 420
καὶ δ᾽ αὖθ᾽ ἡ κυνάμυια ἄγει βροτολοιγὸν Ἄρηα
δηίου ἐκ πολέμοιο κατὰ κλόνον· ἀλλὰ μέτελθε."
ὣς φάτ᾽, Ἀθηναίη δὲ μετέσσυτο, χαῖρε δὲ θυμῷ,
καί ρ᾽ ἐπιεισαμένη πρὸς στήθεα χειρὶ παχείῃ
ἤλασε· τῆς δ᾽ αὐτοῦ λύτο γούνατα καὶ φίλον ἦτορ.
τὼ μὲν ἄρ᾽ ἄμφω κεῖντο ἐπὶ χθονὶ πουλυβοτείρῃ, 426
ἡ δ᾽ ἄρ᾽ ἐπευχομένη ἔπεα πτερόεντ᾽ ἀγόρευε·
"τοιοῦτοι νῦν πάντες, ὅσοι Τρώεσσιν ἀρωγοί,
εἶεν, ὅτ᾽ Ἀργείοισι μαχοίατο θωρηκτῇσιν,
ὧδέ τε θαρσαλέοι καὶ τλήμονες, ὡς Ἀφροδίτη 430
ἦλθεν Ἄρει ἐπίκουρος, ἐμῷ μένει ἀντιόωσα·
τῶ κεν δὴ πάλαι ἄμμες ἐπαυσάμεθα πτολέμοιο,
Ἰλίου ἐκπέρσαντες ἐϋκτίμενον πτολίεθρον."
ὣς φάτο, μείδησεν δὲ θεὰ λευκώλενος Ἥρη.
αὐτὰρ Ἀπόλλωνα προσέφη κρείων ἐνοσίχθων· 435
"Φοῖβε, τίη δὴ νῶι διέσταμεν; οὐδὲ ἔοικεν
ἀρξάντων ἑτέρων· τὸ μὲν αἴσχιον, αἴ κ᾽ ἀμαχητὶ
ἴομεν Οὐλυμπόνδε, Διὸς ποτὶ χαλκοβατὲς δῶ.
ἄρχε· σὺ γὰρ γενεῆφι νεώτερος· οὐ γὰρ ἐμοί γε

καλόν, ἐπεὶ πρότερος γενόμην καὶ πλείονα οἶδα. 440
νηπύτι', ὡς ἄνοον κραδίην ἔχες· οὐδέ νυ τῶν περ
μέμνηαι, ὅσα δὴ πάθομεν κακὰ Ἴλιον ἀμφὶς
μοῦνοι νῶι θεῶν, ὅτ᾽ ἀγήνορι Λαομέδοντι
πὰρ Διὸς ἐλθόντες θητεύσαμεν εἰς ἐνιαυτὸν
μισθῷ ἔπι ῥητῷ· ὁ δὲ σημαίνων ἐπέτελλεν. 445
ἦ τοι ἐγὼ Τρώεσσι πόλιν πέρι τεῖχος ἔδειμα
εὐρύ τε καὶ μάλα καλόν, ἵν᾽ ἄρρηκτος πόλις εἴη·
Φοῖβε, σὺ δ᾽ εἰλίποδας ἕλικας βοῦς βουκολέεσκες
Ἴδης ἐν κνημοῖσι πολυπτύχου ὑληέσσης.
ἀλλ᾽ ὅτε δὴ μισθοῖο τέλος πολυγηθέες Ὧραι 450
ἐξέφερον, τότε νῶι βιήσατο μισθὸν ἅπαντα
Λαομέδων ἔκπαγλος, ἀπειλήσας δ᾽ ἀπέπεμπε.
σὺν μὲν ὅ γ᾽ ἠπείλησε πόδας καὶ χεῖρας ὕπερθε
δήσειν, καὶ περάαν νήσων ἔπι τηλεδαπάων·
στεῦτο δ᾽ ὅ γ᾽ ἀμφοτέρων ἀπολεψέμεν οὔατα χαλκῷ.
νῶι δέ τ᾽ ἄψορροι κίομεν κεκοτηότι θυμῷ, 456
μισθοῦ χωόμενοι, τὸν ὑποστὰς οὐκ ἐτέλεσσε.
τοῦ δὴ νῦν λαοῖσι φέρεις χάριν, οὐδὲ μεθ᾽ ἡμέων
πειρᾷ, ὥς κε Τρῶες ὑπερφίαλοι ἀπόλωνται
πρόχνυ κακῶς σὺν παισὶ καὶ αἰδοίῃσ᾽ ἀλόχοισι." 460
τὸν δ᾽ αὖτε προσέειπε ἄναξ ἑκάεργος Ἀπόλλων·
" ἐννοσίγαι᾽, οὐκ ἄν με σαόφρονα μυθήσαιο
ἔμμεναι, εἰ δὴ σοί γε βροτῶν ἕνεκα πτολεμίξω
δειλῶν, οἳ φύλλοισι ἐοικότες ἄλλοτε μέν τε
ζαφλεγέες τελέθουσιν, ἀρούρης καρπὸν ἔδοντες, 465
ἄλλοτε δὲ φθινύθουσιν ἀκήριοι. ἀλλὰ τάχιστα
παυσώμεσθα μάχης· οἱ δ᾽ αὐτοὶ δηριαάσθων."
ὣς ἄρα φωνήσας πάλιν ἐτράπετ᾽· αἴδετο γάρ ῥα
πατροκασιγνήτοιο μιγήμεναι ἐν παλάμῃσι.

τὸν δὲ κασιγνήτη μάλα νείκεσε, πότνια θηρῶν,   470
Ἄρτεμις ἀγροτέρη, καὶ ὀνειδέϊον φάτο μῦθον·
" φεύγεις δή, ἑκάεργε, Ποσειδάωνι δὲ νίκην
πᾶσαν ἐπέτρεψας, μέλεον δέ οἱ εὖχος ἔδωκας·
νηπύτιε, τί νυ τόξον ἔχεις ἀνεμώλιον αὔτως ;
μή σευ νῦν ἔτι πατρὸς ἐνὶ μεγάροισιν ἀκούσω   475
εὐχομένου, ὡς τὸ πρὶν ἐν ἀθανάτοισι θεοῖσιν,
ἄντα Ποσειδάωνος ἐναντίβιον πολεμίξειν."
    ὣς φάτο, τὴν δ' οὔ τι προσέφη ἑκάεργος Ἀπόλλων,
ἀλλὰ χολωσαμένη Διὸς αἰδοίη παράκοιτις
νείκεσεν ἰοχέαιραν ὀνειδείοις ἐπέεσσιν·   480
" πῶς δὲ σὺ νῦν μέμονας, κύον ἀδδεές, ἀντί' ἐμεῖο
στήσεσθαι; χαλεπή τοι ἐγὼ μένος ἀντιφέρεσθαι
τοξοφόρῳ περ ἐούσῃ, ἐπεί σε λέοντα γυναιξὶ
Ζεὺς θῆκεν καὶ ἔδωκε κατακτάμεν ἥν κ' ἐθέλησθα.
ἦ τοι βέλτερόν ἐστι κατ' οὔρεα θῆρας ἐναίρειν   485
ἀγροτέρας τ' ἐλάφους ἢ κρείσσοσι ἶφι μάχεσθαι.
εἰ δ' ἐθέλεις πολέμοιο δαήμεναι, ὄφρ' ἐῢ εἰδῇς,
ὅσσον φερτέρη εἴμ', ὅτι μοι μένος ἀντιφερίζεις."
    ἦ ῥα, καὶ ἀμφοτέρας ἐπὶ καρπῷ χεῖρας ἔμαρπτε
σκαιῇ, δεξιτερῇ δ' ἄρ' ἀπ' ὤμων αἴνυτο τόξα,   490
αὐτοῖσιν δ' ἄρ' ἔθεινε παρ' οὔατα μειδιόωσα
ἐντροπαλιζομένην· ταχέες δ' ἔκπιπτον ὀϊστοί.
δακρυόεσσα δ' ὕπαιθα θεὰ φύγεν ὥς τε πέλεια,
ἥ ῥά θ' ὑπ' ἴρηκος κοίλην εἰσέπτατο πέτρην,
χηραμόν· οὐδ' ἄρα τῇ γε ἁλώμεναι αἴσιμον ἦεν·   495
ὣς ἡ δακρυόεσσα φύγεν, λίπε δ' αὐτόθι τόξα.
Λητὼ δὲ προσέειπε διάκτορος Ἀργεϊφόντης·
    " Λητοῖ, ἐγὼ δέ τοι οὔ τι μαχήσομαι· ἀργαλέον γὰρ
πληκτίζεσθ' ἀλόχοισι Διὸς νεφεληγερέταο·

ἀλλὰ μάλα πρόφρασσα μετ' ἀθανάτοισι θεοῖσιν 500
εὔχεσθαι ἐμὲ νικῆσαι κρατερῆφι βίηφιν."
ὣς ἄρ' ἔφη, Λητὼ δὲ συναίνυτο καμπύλα τόξα
πεπτεῶτ' ἄλλυδις ἄλλα μετὰ στροφάλιγγι κονίης.
ἡ μὲν τόξα λαβοῦσα πάλιν κίε θυγατέρος ἧς·
ἡ δ' ἄρ' Ὄλυμπον ἵκανε, Διὸς ποτὶ χαλκοβατὲς δῶ,
δακρυόεσσα δὲ πατρὸς ἐφέζετο γούνασι κούρη, 506
ἀμφὶ δ' ἄρ' ἀμβρόσιος ἑανὸς τρέμε· τὴν δὲ προτὶ οἱ
εἷλε πατὴρ Κρονίδης, καὶ ἀνείρετο ἡδὺ γελάσσας·
" τίς νύ σε τοιάδ' ἔρεξε, φίλον τέκος, Οὐρανιώνων
μαψιδίως, ὡσεί τι κακὸν ῥέζουσαν ἐνωπῇ ;" 510
τὸν δ' αὖτε προσέειπεν ἐϋστέφανος κελαδεινή·
" σή μ' ἄλοχος στυφέλιξε, πάτερ, λευκώλενος Ἥρη,
ἐξ ἧς ἀθανάτοισιν ἔρις καὶ νεῖκε' ἐφῆπται."
ὣς οἱ μὲν τοιαῦτα πρὸς ἀλλήλους ἀγόρευον,
αὐτὰρ Ἀπόλλων Φοῖβος ἐδύσετο Ἴλιον ἱρήν· 515
μέμβλετο γάρ οἱ τεῖχος ἐϋδμήτοιο πόληος,
μὴ Δαναοὶ πέρσειαν ὑπερμόρον ἤματι κείνῳ.
οἱ δ' ἄλλοι πρὸς Ὄλυμπον ἴσαν θεοὶ αἰὲν ἐόντες,
οἱ μὲν χωόμενοι, οἱ δὲ μέγα κυδιόωντες· 519
κὰδ δ' ἷζον παρὰ πατρὶ κελαινεφεῖ. αὐτὰρ Ἀχιλλεὺς
Τρῶας ὁμῶς αὐτούς τ' ὄλεκεν καὶ μώνυχας ἵππους.
ὡς δ' ὅτε καπνὸς ἰὼν εἰς οὐρανὸν εὐρὺν ἵκηται
ἄστεος αἰθομένοιο, θεῶν δέ ἑ μῆνις ἀνῆκε,
πᾶσι δ' ἔθηκε πόνον, πολλοῖσι δὲ κήδε' ἐφῆκεν,
ὣς Ἀχιλεὺς Τρώεσσι πόνον καὶ κήδε' ἔθηκεν. 525
ἑστήκει δ' ὁ γέρων Πρίαμος θείου ἐπὶ πύργου,
ἐς δ' ἐνόησ' Ἀχιλῆα πελώριον· αὐτὰρ ὑπ' αὐτοῦ
Τρῶες ἄφαρ κλονέοντο πεφυζότες, οὐδέ τις ἀλκὴ
γίγνεθ'· ὁ δ' οἰμώξας, ἀπὸ πύργου βαῖνε χαμᾶζε,

ὀτρύνεων παρὰ τεῖχος ἀγακλεϊτοὺς πυλαωρούς· 530
"πεπταμένας ἐν χερσὶ πύλας ἔχετ', εἰς ὅ κε λαοὶ
ἔλθωσι προτὶ ἄστυ πεφυζότες· ἦ γὰρ Ἀχιλλεὺς
ἐγγὺς ὅδε κλονέων· νῦν οἴω λοίγι' ἔσεσθαι.
αὐτὰρ ἐπεί κ' ἐς τεῖχος ἀναπνεύσωσι ἀλέντες,
αὖτις ἐπανθέμεναι σανίδας πυκινῶς ἀραρυίας· 535
δείδια γὰρ μὴ οὖλος ἀνὴρ ἐς τεῖχος ἄληται."
   ὣς ἔφαθ', οἱ δ' ἄνεσάν τε πύλας καὶ ἀπῶσαν ὀχῆας·
αἱ δὲ πετασθεῖσαι τεῦξαν φάος. αὐτὰρ Ἀπόλλων
ἀντίος ἐξέθορε, Τρώων ἵνα λοιγὸν ἀλάλκοι.
οἱ δ' ἰθὺς πόλιος καὶ τείχεος ὑψηλοῖο, 540
δίψῃ καρχαλέοι, κεκονιμένοι ἐκ πεδίοιο
φεῦγον· ὁ δὲ σφεδανὸν ἔφεπ' ἔγχεϊ· λύσσα δέ οἱ κῆρ
αἰὲν ἔχε κρατερή, μενέαινε δὲ κῦδος ἀρέσθαι.
   ἔνθα κεν ὑψίπυλον Τροίην ἕλον υἷες Ἀχαιῶν,
εἰ μὴ Ἀπόλλων Φοῖβος Ἀγήνορα δῖον ἀνῆκε, 545
φῶτ' Ἀντήνορος υἱὸν ἀμύμονά τε κρατερόν τε.
ἐν μέν οἱ κραδίῃ θάρσος βάλε, πὰρ δέ οἱ αὐτὸς
ἔστη, ὅπως θανάτοιο βαρείας κῆρας ἀλάλκοι,
φηγῷ κεκλιμένος· κεκάλυπτο δ' ἄρ' ἠέρι πολλῇ.
αὐτὰρ ὅ γ' ὡς ἐνόησεν Ἀχιλλῆα πτολίπορθον, 550
ἔστη, πολλὰ δέ οἱ κραδίη πόρφυρε μένοντι·
ὀχθήσας δ' ἄρα εἶπε πρὸς ὃν μεγαλήτορα θυμόν·
   "ὤ μοι ἐγών· εἰ μέν κεν ὑπὸ κρατεροῦ Ἀχιλῆος
φεύγω, τῇ περ οἱ ἄλλοι ἀτυζόμενοι κλονέονται,
αἱρήσει με καὶ ὣς καὶ ἀνάλκιδα δειροτομήσει. 555
εἰ δ' ἂν ἐγὼ τούτους μὲν ὑποκλονέεσθαι ἐάσω
Πηλείδῃ Ἀχιλῆι, ποσὶν δ' ἀπὸ τείχεος ἄλλη
φεύγω πρὸς πεδίον Ἰλήιον, ὄφρ' ἂν ἵκωμαι
Ἴδης τε κνημοὺς κατά τε ῥωπήια δύω·

ἑσπέριος δ' ἂν ἔπειτα λοεσσάμενος ποταμοῖο,   560
ἱδρῶ ἀποψυχθεὶς ποτὶ Ἴλιον ἀπονεοίμην.
ἀλλὰ τίη μοι ταῦτα φίλος διελέξατο θυμός;
μή μ' ἀπαειρόμενον πόλιος πεδίονδε νοήσῃ
καί με μεταΐξας μάρψῃ ταχέεσσι πόδεσσιν.
οὐκέτ' ἔπειτ' ἔσται θάνατον καὶ κῆρας ἀλύξαι·   565
λίην γὰρ κρατερὸς περὶ πάντων ἔστ' ἀνθρώπων.
εἰ δέ κέ οἱ προπάροιθε πόλιος κατεναντίον ἔλθω·—
καὶ γάρ θην τούτῳ τρωτὸς χρὼς ὀξέϊ χαλκῷ,
ἐν δὲ ἴα ψυχή, θνητὸν δέ ἕ φασ' ἄνθρωποι
ἔμμεναι· αὐτάρ οἱ Κρονίδης Ζεὺς κῦδος ὀπάζει."   570
ὣς εἰπὼν Ἀχιλῆα ἀλεὶς μένεν, ἐν δέ οἱ ἦτορ
ἄλκιμον ὡρμᾶτο πτολεμίζειν ἠδὲ μάχεσθαι.
ἠΰτε πάρδαλις εἶσι βαθείης ἐκ ξυλόχοιο
ἀνδρὸς θηρητῆρος ἐναντίον, οὐδέ τι θυμῷ
ταρβεῖ οὐδὲ φοβεῖται, ἐπεί κεν ὑλαγμὸν ἀκούσῃ·   575
εἴ περ γὰρ φθάμενός μιν ἢ οὐτάσῃ ἠὲ βάλησιν,
ἀλλά τε καὶ περὶ δουρὶ πεπαρμένη οὐκ ἀπολήγει
ἀλκῆς, πρίν γ' ἠὲ ξυμβλήμεναι ἠὲ δαμῆναι·
ὣς Ἀντήνορος υἱὸς ἀγαυοῦ, δῖος Ἀγήνωρ,
οὐκ ἔθελεν φεύγειν, πρὶν πειρήσαιτ' Ἀχιλῆος,   580
ἀλλ' ὅ γ' ἄρ' ἀσπίδα μὲν πρόσθ' ἔσχετο πάντοσ' ἐΐσην,
ἐγχείῃ δ' αὐτοῖο τιτύσκετο, καὶ μέγ' ἀΰτει·
"ἦ δή που μάλ' ἔολπας ἐνὶ φρεσί, φαίδιμ' Ἀχιλλεῦ,
ἤματι τῷδε πόλιν πέρσειν Τρώων ἀγερώχων,
νηπύτι'· ἦ τ' ἔτι πολλὰ τετεύξεται ἄλγε' ἐπ' αὐτῇ.   585
ἐν γάρ οἱ πολέες τε καὶ ἄλκιμοι ἀνέρες εἰμέν,
οἳ καὶ πρόσθε φίλων τοκέων ἀλόχων τε καὶ υἱῶν
Ἴλιον εἰρυόμεσθα· σὺ δ' ἐνθάδε πότμον ἐφέψεις,
ὧδ' ἔκπαγλος ἐὼν καὶ θαρσαλέος πολεμιστής."

ἦ ῥα, καὶ ὀξὺν ἄκοντα βαρείης χειρὸς ἀφῆκε, 590
καί ῥ' ἔβαλε κνήμην ὑπὸ γούνατος οὐδ' ἀφάμαρτεν.
ἀμφὶ δέ μιν κνημὶς νεοτεύκτου κασσιτέροιο
σμερδαλέον κονάβησε· πάλιν δ' ἀπὸ χαλκὸς ὄρουσε
βλημένου, οὐδ' ἐπέρησε, θεοῦ δ' ἠρύκακε δῶρα.
Πηλεΐδης δ' ὡρμήσατ' Ἀγήνορος ἀντιθέοιο 595
δεύτερος· οὐδέ τ' ἔασεν Ἀπόλλων κῦδος ἀρέσθαι,
ἀλλά μιν ἐξήρπαξε, κάλυψε δ' ἄρ' ἠέρι πολλῇ,
ἡσύχιον δ' ἄρα μιν πολέμου ἔκπεμπε νέεσθαι.
αὐτὰρ ὁ Πηλεΐωνα δόλῳ ἀποέργαθε λαοῦ·
αὐτῷ γὰρ ἑκάεργος Ἀγήνορι πάντα ἐοικὼς 600
ἔστη πρόσθε ποδῶν· ὁ δ' ἐπέσσυτο ποσσὶ διώκειν.
εἷος ὁ τὸν πεδίοιο διώκετο πυροφόροιο,
τρέψας πὰρ ποταμὸν βαθυδινήεντα Σκάμανδρον,
τυτθὸν ὑπεκπροθέοντα· δόλῳ δ' ἄρα θέλγεν Ἀπόλλων,
ὡς αἰεὶ ἔλποιτο κιχήσεσθαι ποσὶ οἷσι— 605
τόφρ' ἄλλοι Τρῶες πεφοβημένοι ἦλθον ὁμίλῳ
ἀσπάσιοι προτὶ ἄστυ, πόλις δ' ἔμπλητο ἀλέντων.
οὐδ' ἄρα τοί γ' ἔτλαν πόλιος καὶ τείχεος ἐκτὸς
μεῖναι ἔτ' ἀλλήλους, καὶ γνώμεναι ὅς τε πεφεύγοι
ὅς τ' ἔθαν' ἐν πολέμῳ· ἀλλ' ἐσσυμένως ἐσέχυντο 610
ἐς πόλιν, ὅν τινα τῶν γε πόδες καὶ γοῦνα σαώσαι.

NOTES

The references marked § are to sections in the Introduction.

1. **πόρον.** For the use of the case without a preposition see § 20 (*a*).

ἷξον. The subject is the fleeing Trojans. For the 'mixed' aorist, with a 'weak' stem but 'strong' ending, see § 13 (*b*).

ἐυρρεῖος. The position of the breathing shows that ἐυ- is not here treated as a diphthong.

2. **ὅν.** For the origin of the relative ὅς see § 16.

τέκετο. For the omission of the augment cf. δίωκε (3), φοβέοντο (4), etc. and § 13 (*h*); for the voice see § 18 (*a*).

Ζεύς as the sky god may be regarded as the parent of rivers because they owe their origin to rain. Cf. Σκάμανδρε διοτρεφές (223), διιπετέος ποταμοῖο (268).

3. **διατμήξας.** Supply Achilles as subject.

τούς. For the Homeric use of ὁ, ἡ, τό, see § 16.

πεδίονδε. For the ending -δε see § 26.

4. **φοβέοντο.** Words are constantly left uncontracted in Homer, § 10.

5. **ἤματι.** For the case see § 21 (*b*).

τῷ = *that*, not *the*, § 16.

6. **τῇ** takes up ᾗ (4). For the case see § 21 (*b*).

ῥ'...γε. For the force of these and other particles see § 5.

πεφυζότες apparently = πεφευγότες. It is only found in *Iliad* xx and xxi. Monro regards it as formed from a noun φύζα without the intervention of any tense-stem and compares κεκοπώς (xiii 60) from κόπος and δεδουπότος (xxiii 679) from δοῦπος.

7. **ἐρυκέμεν.** For the form of the infinitive see § 15 (*b*) and for the construction, § 18 (*b*).

8. **εἰλεῦντο.** For the contraction see § 10.

9. **ἐν.** Adverb, see § 23.

πατάγῳ. For the case see § 21 (*c*).

10. **ἀμφὶ περί.** For the combination of prepositions see § 24.

μεγάλ'. For the adverbial use of the neut. accus. of an adjective see § 20 (b).

ἀλαλητῷ. For construction cf. πατάγῳ (9).

11. ἔννεον. Leaf thinks this = ἐ·σνεϝ·ον, not ἐν-ένεον, because ἐν compounded with verbs usually denotes *into* and not *in*.

12. ὥς. For Homeric similes see § 28. Fires are said to be still used in Cyprus to drive locusts from corn-fields.

ὑπό, rather *from under* than *by*; cf. 22.

13. φευγέμεναι, cf. note on ἐρυκέμεν (7).

φλέγει probably transitive, πῦρ being in apposition to τό, = *this— the tireless fire—consumes them*.

15. ὥς. Notice the difference between ὡς with and without an accent.

16. ἐπιμίξ. For this ending of an adverb cf. ἅπαξ, ὀδάξ.

ἵππων. For the case see § 22 (a).

17. ὁ, *he*, not *the*.

αὐτοῦ. Adverb.

18. μυρίκῃσιν. For case see § 21 (b) and cf. 549.

19. κακά. Not in a moral sense.

φρεσί. For case see § 21 (b).

20. ἐπιστροφάδην. For this form of adverb cf. ἐπιγράβδην (166), ἀμβολάδην (364) and § 23.

22. ὑπό, cf. 12 (note).

25. κατά. With ῥέεθρα.

26. κρημνούς. For case see § 23, s.v. ὑπό.

χεῖρας. Adverbial accusative, see § 20 (b).

29. τούς, *these*, § 16.

30. ἱμᾶσι. Instrumental, § 21 (c).

31. τούς. In Attic a relative pronoun would have been used; see § 16.

φορέεσκον. For tense see § 13 (a).

32. κατάγειν. For construction cf. ἐρυκέμεν (7).

κοίλας. A stock-epithet of ships, § 4.

35. ποταμοῦ. Notice genit. in -ου, though -οιο in 1, 25, 27.

τόν, cf. τούς (31).

36. ἐκ, with ἀλωῆς, cf. 25.

37. ἐννύχιος. Adjective = adverb. Cf. ἐσπέριος (560), δεύτερος (596), ἀσπάσιοι (607) and § 23.

ἐρινεὸν...ὅρπηκας. Accus. of the Whole and the Part:
see § 20 (c).

39. **τῷ.** Dat. of Disadvantage, § 21 (a).

ἤλυθε. N.B. ἦλθε in 57.

40. **Λῆμνον,** cf. πόρον (1 note). In 58 ἐς is inserted.

ἐπέρασσε. For the doubling of the consonant cf. ὀτίσσω (30)
and § 8.

41. **νηυσίν.** Either locative (*in ships*), or instrumental (*by ships*),
§ 21 (b) and (c).

υἱὸς Ἰήσονος. Euneus, king of Lemnos. N.B. in 34 υἱεῖ (from
υἱεύς).

42. **κεῖθεν.** For the ending -θεν see § 26.

44. **ὑπεκπροφυγών,** cf. note on ἀμφὶ περί (10).

45. **ἤματα.** Accus. of Time, § 20 (b).

θυμόν, cf. χεῖρας (26 note).

οἶσι. From ὅς (possessive).

ᶠ **φίλοισιν.** Usually classed as a locative (*among his friends*), but
might be instrumental: see § 21 (b) and (c).

46. **δυωδεκάτῃ.** For the case cf. ἤματι (5). Notice that ἤματα
is neuter and therefore this word cannot agree with ἤματι understood, though it could with ἡμέρᾳ. Cf. *Od.* x 80 ἐξῆμαρ...πλέομεν...
ἑβδομάτῃ δ' ἱκόμεσθα.

47. **χερσίν.** Probably dat. of Advantage, not 'governed' by
ἔμβαλεν, but cf. § 25.

48. **πέμψειν.** The future infin. is constantly found after μέλλω.

εἰς, sc. some such word as δῶμα and compare *Ventum erat ad
Vestae* (Horace), and such English phrases as *to go to S. Paul's.*
N.B. ἐς in 43.

νέεσθαι may depend on ἐθέλοντα or be an epexegetic (i.e. explanatory) infinitive after πέμψειν, § 18 (b).

49. **ποδάρκης.** A stock-epithet of Achilles; cf. 265.

51. **ἀπό.** Adverb, § 23.

χαμαί. We should rather have expected χαμᾶζε (*to the ground*),
but see § 25.

52. **ὑπό.** Adverb, § 23.

53. **δ'** here is not needed, for ἄτερ...ἐδάμνα is merely parenthe-
tical. This use of δέ (=*then*) is called δέ in the apodosis, because it
is found sometimes in the result clause of a conditional sentence.

πρός with accus. is often found instead of the simple dative after verbs of speaking.

54. ὁρῶμαι. For voice cf. τέκετο (2).

57. οἶον. Adverbial accus. § 20 (b).

ὕπο. N.B. accent thrown back on to first syllable to show that the preposition (or rather adverb) is following the word which it qualifies.

59. πόντος ἁλός, cf. Verg. *Aen.* x 377 *maris pontus.*

ὅ. In a relative sense; cf. τούς (31).

60. ἀκωκῆς. For case see § 22 (b).

61. γεύσεται may be indic. but as ἄγε constantly is joined with subj. it is more probably aor. subj. in an imperative sense; cf. § 15 (a).

ἴδωμαι, cf. ὁρῶμαι (54).

63. κατά. Adverb, § 23.

64. οἱ. For case see § 21 (a). In Homer the pronoun ἕ is usually non-reflexive, but its possessive ὅς (ἑός) is usually reflexive.

65. γούνων. For case see § 22 (b).

περί. Adverb, § 23.

θυμῷ, cf. φρεσί (19).

67. ἀνέσχετο. For voice cf. τέκετο (2).

68. γούνων, cf. 65.

70. χροός. For case see § 22 (a).

71. τῇ, § 16.

γούνων may be taken with ἑλών (cf. 65) or more probably with ἑλλίσσετο. See § 22 (b).

ἑλλίσσετο. Notice the doubling of λ, § 8.

73. προσηύδα. For the double accus. see § 20 (c).

74. Ἀχιλεῦ. Hitherto spelt -λλ-, § 8.

αἴδεό...ἐλέησον. Notice change of tense.

75. αἰδοίοιο. Suppliants were regarded as under the protection of Ζεὺς Ἱκέσιος.

76. πρώτῳ, i.e. among Greeks.

77. ἤματι, cf. 5.

78. ἄνευθεν, with πατρός.

80. λύμην. The payment seems to be that made by Eetion in 42.

82. ἐν, § 25.

83. Διί. Perhaps dat. of Agent, § 21 (c), but ἀπεχθέσθαι may = *to be an object of hatred.*

85. "Αλταο..."Αλτεω, § 12. Probably 86 is a later addition.

86. Δελέγεσσι. The dative with words like ἀνάσσει has been explained as locative, but it may be dat. of Advantage.

φιλοπτολέμοισι. For the -πτ- see § 8.

88. ἔχε, i.e. as wife.

89. τῆs. For case see § 22 (c).

94. σῆσι, though τεῆσ' in 82.

96. ὅs, though ὁ in 59.

99. μοι, § 21 (a).

101. τί. Adverbial accusative, see § 20 (b).

103. ὅστις...φύγῃ. For omission of ἄν see § 18 (d). φύγῃσι is the form used in 296.

104. Ἰλίου scans Ἰλίοο, which is probably the right reading, § 12.

προπάροιθεν, cf. ἀμφὶ περί (10 note).

ἐν χερσί, § 25.

105. πέρι. Adverb, hence accent, § 23. This is customary also with ἄπο and perhaps ὕπο (Monro).

106. φίλος. For case see § 19.

τίη. See § 20 (b).

107. ὅ = ὅs, cf. 59.

σέο, but ἐμεῖο in 112.

πολλόν. Adverbial accusative, § 20 (b).

109. πατρός. For the case see § 22 (c) and cf. 89.

110. ἔπι. The accent denotes that it = ἔπεστι.

112. ὁππότε...ἔληται. For omission of ἄν cf. 103.

Ἀρει. Either locative or instrumental dative. Ares is of course used here for war cf. Ceres, Venus, Bacchus etc. in Latin.

ἐκ. Adverb, § 23.

113. νευρῆφιν. For the ending see § 26.

114. φάτο. For voice cf. τέκετο (2).

αὐτοῦ. Adverb.

φίλον ἦτορ. A favourite phrase. Cf. 201, 389, 425.

116. ἀμφοτέρας, though χεῖρε is dual: see § 17.

117. οἱ. Dative of Disadvantage, § 21 (a).

119. ἐκ. Adverb, § 23.

120. ποδός, cf. 68.

φέρεσθαι, cf. 7 and § 18 (b).

121. οἱ. With ἐπευχόμενος : perhaps dat. of Disadvantage.

122. **σ' ὠτειλὴν αἷμα.** For the triple accusative see § 20 (*c*).

124. **λεχέεσσι.** See note on 11 and § 25.

125. **εἴσω.** Probably with κόλπον, though found with a gen. in *Od.* viii 290.

128. **φθείρεσθ'.** Notice plural.

κιχείομεν, cf. δαείω (61).

'Ιλίου, cf. note on 104.

131. **δηθά...ἱερεύετε,** cf. Latin use of *jamdudum* with present tense.

132. **ἐν.** See § 25.

ἵππους. Herodotus mentions sacrifices of horses by Persians.

133. **ὀλέεσθε...μόρον.** Cognate accus., § 20 (*b*).

134. **τίσετε.** Subjunctive, § 15.

135. **θοῇσιν.** A stock-epithet for ships.

136. **ἔφη,** though φάτο in 114.

137. **πόνοιο.** For case see § 22 (*c*).

138. **Τρώεσσι.** Dat. of Advantage, § 21 (*a*).

140. **'Αστεροπαίῳ.** Probably dat. of Disadvantage. See § 23 as to compound verbs.

κατακτάμεναι μενεαίνων, cf. 33.

145. **οἱ.** Dat. of Advantage, § 21 (*a*).

ἐν. See § 25.

146. **αἰζηῶν.** Perhaps gen. absolute, but probably gen. of Aim; cf. μισθοῦ (457) and see § 22 (*e*).

148. **ἐπ' ἀλλήλοισιν ἰόντες.** See § 25.

149. **πρότερος,** cf. note on ἐννύχιος (37).

150. **εἶς** is read in nine places in Homer, but there is only one in which the metre would not allow ἐσσί—probably the correct Homeric form (Monro).

ὅ. Really an adverbial accus. of the relative pronoun (=*in respect that...*); see § 20 (*b*).

156. Cf. 81.

157. **εὐρύ.** Adverbial accus. § 20 (*b*).

158. Found also in ii 850.

161. Cf. 67.

162. **ἀμαρτῇ.** Perhaps a relic of the old instrumental case, § 12.

δούρασιν taken up by ἑτέρῳ...ἑτέρῳ βάλε.

164. **διαπρό,** § 24.

165. **χρυσός.** Mentioned perhaps as most precious part of metal shield: the plur. **δῶρα** may denote the bits of gold (Leaf), but it seems more probable that the poet is thinking also of other parts of the armour.

ἐρύκακε. Notice the peculiar formation of the aorist, § 13 (*d*).

θεοῖο, i.e. Hephaestus.

166. **τῷ,** *that,* § 16.

μιν πῆχυν...βάλε, cf. 37 (note).

ἐπιγράβδην, cf. 20 (note).

167. **ἥ.** Notice the gender: the poet has been speaking of a **δόρυ** (neut.) but may be thinking of **αἰχμή** (fem.); cf. 46 (note).

168. **γαίη.** Locative, § 23 (compound verbs).

χροός, cf. 70.

169. **δεύτερος.** For adverbial use cf. **ἐννύχιος** (37 note).

170. The line is almost a repetition of 140.

ἐφῆκε, but **ἀφέηκεν** in 115. In 177 we find **μεθῆκε.**

171. **τοῦ.** For case see § 22 (*e*).

172. For **μεσσοπαγές** there is another reading **μεσσοπαλές** (=*quivering to its centre*).

ὄχθης. For case see § 23 (s.v. **κατά**).

μείλινον, though **μελίην** in 169.

174. **οἱ.** See § 25.

175. **χειρὶ παχείῃ.** A favourite phrase, cf. 403, 424.

177. **βίης,** § 22 (*c*).

τό, § 16.

θυμῷ, § 21 (*b*).

179. Leaf inserts **ἕ** after **ἀλλά.**

180. **γαστέρα...μιν,** cf. 37, but notice that here the part precedes the whole.

ἐκ. Adverb, § 23.

181. Notice the alliteration and that **χαμαί** is used where we might expect **χαμᾶζε**; cf. 51.

τὸν...ὄσσε, cf. 37.

182. **ἐνί,** § 25.

185. **ποταμοῖο.** Gen. of Origin; see § 23 (compound verbs).

186. **ποταμοῦ** (N.B. **ποταμοῖο** in 185) may be gen. of Origin but perhaps more probably possessive, as also **Διός** in 187.

γένος, γενεήν (187). Adverbial accus., § 20 (b).

εὐρὺ ῥέοντος, cf. 157.

188. πολλοῖσι, cf. 86 (note).

189. ὅ, § 16.

190. τῷ perhaps should be written τῶ as the old instrumental case, cf. 162.

191. ποταμοῖο = γενεῆς ποταμοῖο. This compressed construction is called Brachylogy.

192. πάρα. Notice accent thrown back because it = πάρεστι; cf. ἔπι (110).

τι. Adverbial accus., § 20 (b).

198. ὅς, § 16.

δείδοικε, but δειδιότες (24) and δείδια (536).

199. ὅτ'...σμαραγήσῃ. No ἄν, § 18 (d).

ἀπ' οὐρανόθεν, § 26.

200. ἤ. Verb.

201. κατ' αὐτόθι. Both adverbs.

204. ἐπινεφρίδιον. New Zealand parrots are said to have a taste for the same part of a sheep.

205. βῆ...ἰέναι. A phrase found often in Homer. ἰέναι seems to be an epexegetic infinitive, § 18 (b).

207. τὸν ἄριστον, that most famous man, § 16.

208. ὕπο. Notice accent; cf. 57 (note).

214. περί, with ἀνδρῶν, § 23.

215. ἀνδρῶν, but ἀνέρι in 213.

217. ἐξ ἐμέθεν, § 26.

κάτα. Notice accent; cf. 57 (note).

218. μοι. Probably dat. of Disadvantage, § 21 (a).

νεκύων. Gen. of Material, § 22 (a).

219. τι, § 20 (b).

223. Perhaps ironical.

διοτρεφές, cf. 2 (note).

224. Notice the double πρίν: in Attic we often find πρότερον... πρίν.

225. Ἕκτορι. After ἀντιβίην.

226. ἤ...ἤ, cf. § 5.

δαμάσσεται. Aor. subj. The clause seems to be an indirect question depending on πειρηθῆναι, to try whether he will conquer me *or I him*, the dependent sentences being equivalent to a kind of object or adverbial accus. to πειρηθῆναι, cf. 62. For κέν with subj. cf. § 18 (*d*).

227. **Τρώεσσιν**, § 23 (compound verbs).

230. **ὅ**, cf. 150 (note).

πόλλ'. Adverbial accus. § 20 (*b*).

231. **Τρωσί**, though Τρώεσσιν in 227. For construction see § 23 (compound verbs).

233. **ἥ**, cf. 200.

μέσσῳ, § 25.

241. **ἐν**, § 25.

242. **εἶχε**, *was able.*

243. **ἐριποῦσα** from ἐρείπω as λιποῦσα from λείπω.

247. **πεδίοιο.** Gen. of Space, § 22 (*d*).

ποσί, though πόδεσσιν in 241, ποσσίν in 269.

πέτεσθαι. Epexegetic, § 18 (*b*).

249. **ἀκροκελαινιόων.** Notice assimilation, § 10.

παύσειε πόνοιο κ.τ.λ., cf. 137.

251. **ἐπί** should probably be ἔπι for ὅσον ἔπι = ἐφ' ὅσον with which γίνεται may be supplied; cf. xv 358 (Leaf).

252. **τοῦ**, *that*, § 16.

255. **σμερδάλεον.** Adverbial accus., § 20 (*b*).

256. **ὄπισθε**, but in 129 ὄπιθεν.

ὀρυμαγδῷ, cf. πατάγῳ (9).

257. **ὅτ'...ἡγεμονεύῃ.** No ἄν, § 18 (*d*).

258. Take **ὕδατι** after ἡγεμονεύῃ and **ῥόον** as accus. of Space.

259. **χερσί.** Locative or Instrum. dat., § 21 (*b*).

ἀμάρης, after ἐξ.

260. **τοῦ**, *this*, § 16.

ὑπό. Adverb.

261. **ὀχλεῦνται**, cf. 8 (note).

262. **τὸν ἄγοντα**, *him* (§ 16) *as he guides it.*

265. **ὀρμήσειε.** Opt. of indefinite frequency.

268. **διιπετέος**, cf. 2 (note).

μιν...ὤμους, § 20 (*c*).

270. **θυμῷ**, § 21 (*b*).

ὑπό. Adverb, cf. 52.

271. **ὕπαιθα**, cf. 255: here obviously an adverb.

ποδοῖιν. Dat. of Disadvantage, § 21 (a).

272. οὐρανὸν εὐρύν, cf. 267.

273. ὡς. Exclamatory—*to think how*.

274. πάθοιμι. A wish—*would that I might suffer something* (i.e. *die*).

275. τόσον. Adverbial accus., § 20 (b); in 321 τόσσην.

276. ἀλλά=ὅσον.

279. ὡς...ὄφελ'. One of the ways of expressing a wish in Greek: perhaps literally *to think how Hector ought to have slain me*, cf. 273 (note).

280. τῷ, *in that case*, cf. 190 (note).

283. ὅν...ἀποέρσῃ. No ἄν, § 18 (d).

χειμῶνι. For case see § 21 (b).

284. φάτο, but ἔφατο (277).

τῷ. Probably dat. of Advantage, § 21 (a).

285. δέμας. Adverbial accus., § 20 (b).

287. τοῖσι. Leaf suggests that the plural (though Poseidon is speaking only to Achilles) is due to the fact that this is merely the repetition of a favourite phrase in Homer: could not the word however mean *for them both* (i.e. Poseidon himself and Athene)?

288. τι, § 20 (b).

291. τοι certainly seems here to be the pronoun, as also in 297.

294. πρίν...πρίν, cf. 224.

πτολέμοιο, § 22 (c).

295. κατά, with τείχεα.

Ἰλιόφι, seems here to be a genitive: see § 26.

296. Ἕκτορι. Probably dat. of Disadvantage, § 21 (a).

θυμὸν ἀπούρας, cf. 179.

297. ἴμεν. The infinitive used for a command, as often in Homer, § 18 (c).

299. μέγα. Adverbial accus., § 20 (b).

300. τό, *it*, § 16.

ὕδατος, § 22 (a).

301. δαικταμένων αἰζηῶν, cf. 146.

302. πλῶον. Notice concord, § 17.

ὑψόσε...ἐπήδα, cf. 269.

304. εὐρὺ ῥέων, cf. 157.

305. **τὸ ὃν μένος,** *that his might,* § 16.

306. **Πηλείωνι.** Probably dat. of Disadvantage, § 21 (*a*). N.B. Πηλείδη in 288.

311. **ἐμπίπληθι.** For form see § 14 and for construction § 22 (*a*). Notice ἵστη is the form used in 313.

314. **παύσομεν.** Subjunctive, § 15 (*a*).

315. **μέμονεν,** though μεμαώς (68); cf. γέγονα and γέγαα from γίγνομαι.

ἶσα. Adverbial accus., § 20 (*b*).

316. **τι,** qualifies χραισμησέμεν, § 20 (*b*).

317. **τὰ τεύχεα καλὰ τά...,** *those arms, the glorious ones, which....*

318. **κάδ.** Adverb.

320. **οἱ.** Dat. of Advantage, § 21 (*a*).

321. **οἱ** (as also in 322). Dat. of Disadvantage, § 21 (*a*).

322. **αὐτοῦ,** *there.*

τι, § 20 (*b*).

μιν. To suppose that the corpse raised his own barrow is awkward. It looks as if the word were object of τυμβοχοῆσαι.

323. **ὅτε...θάπτωσιν.** No ἄν, § 18 (*d*).

324. **ἧ,** verb.

Ἀχιλῆι. Dat. of Disadvantage; see § 23 (compound verbs).

327. **κατά.** Adverb.

328. **μέγ'.** Adverbial accus., § 20 (*b*).

331. **ὅρσεο.** Mixed aorist; cf. ἷξον (1, note).

335. **ἐξ ἁλόθεν,** § 26.

336. **Τρώων,** goes with κεφαλάς and not with ἀπό (adverb, or possibly here separated from κῆαι by tmesis).

338. **ἐν.** Adverb.

ἵει πυρί seems = καῖε.

341. **φθέγξομ'.** Subjunctive, § 15 (*a*).

σχεῖν. Infinitive of command, cf. 297 (note).

344. **κατ' αὐτόθ',** cf. 201 (note). MS. reading is αὐτόν (= *river*?).

347. **ἀγξηράνῃ.** No ἄν, § 18 (*d*).

ὅστις ἐθείρῃ. No ἄν, § 18 (*d*).

348. **κάδ.** Adverb.

352. **τά.** Relative, § 16.

353. **οἱ,** *those.* Leaf prefers to read οἵ (*who*).

356. ἲς ποταμοῖο, *might of the river*, i.e. *the mighty river*; cf. σθένος Ὠκεανοῖο (195).

ἐκ. Adverb, *out he spake*.

358. φλεγέθοντι. With σοι.

359. ἔριδος, § 22 (c).

360. ἐξελάσειε. A wish.

ἔριδος. Partitive gen., § 22 (b).

361. ἀνά. Adverb.

364. ἀμβολάδην, cf. 20 (note).

ὑπό. Adverb.

367. βίηφι, § 26, perhaps a genitive (cf. 295 and 356), or else instrumental.

368. πολλά. Adverbial accus., § 20 (b).

369. τίπτε, § 20 (b).

κήδειν. Probably epexegetic infin., § 18 (b).

370. ἄλλων = πάντων, according to the well-known Greek idiom, copied by Milton in *Adam the goodliest of men since born his sons, fairest of her daughters Eve.*

τόσον. Adverbial accus., § 20 (b). Notice the single σ though in 371 ὅσσον and also ὅσοι.

371. οἱ, *those.*

373. ἐπί. Adverb, *over and above.*

374. ἐπί. Perhaps with Τρώεσσιν (= *in the case of*), cf. 585, or possibly separated by tmesis from ἀλεξήσειν.

377. λευκώλενος. A stock-epithet; cf. 418, 434, 512.

378. Cf. 330.

380. θεόν. Object of στυφελίζειν.

381. θεσπιδαὲς πῦρ, cf. 342.

382. ῥέεθρα. Accus. of Space, § 23 (compound verbs).

383. οἱ...παυσάσθην, § 17.

387. Cf. 9.

388. ἀμφί. Adverb.

389. Οὐλύμπῳ. For case see § 21 (b).

φίλον ἦτορ, cf. 114.

390. ὁρᾶτο, cf. 54 (note).

392. Ἀθηναίῃ. Probably dat. of Disadvantage, § 23 (compound verbs). N.B. Ἀθήνη in 284.

397. οὐτάμεναι, sc. με.

P. H.

398. **ἐμεῦ**. Probably gen. of Aim, § 22. N.B. ἐμεῖο (112), ἐμέθεν (217).

διά. Adverb.

399. **τῶ**, cf. 190 (note).

402. **τῇ**, cf. 6.

405. **ἔμμεναι**. For construction see § 18 (*b*).

οὖρον, perhaps a trace of the old common field system (Leaf); cf. Verg. *Aen.* xii 896 *saxum antiquum ingens campo quod forte jacebat limes agro positus litem ut discerneret arvis.*

409. Cf. 121, 419, 427.

411. **ἔμεναι**, but ἔμμεναι (405).

ὅτι, cf. 150 (note).

412. **τῆς**, *thy*. Leaf suggests that the reading should be ἧς, because the possessive ὅς was once used freely of all persons.

416. **χειρός**, § 22.

417. **πυκνά**. Adverbial accus., § 20 (*b*).

421. **δ'** = δή.

ἥ, *that*.

423. **θυμῷ**, § 21 (*b*).

425. Largely a repetition of 114.

426. **τῶ...κεῖντο**, cf. 383 and § 17.

429. **εἶεν**. A wish: the mood probably influences that of μαχοίατο.

432. **τῶ**, cf. 190 (note).

438. **ἴομεν**. Subjunctive, § 15 (*a*).

441. **ὡς**, cf. 273 (note).

442. **πάθομεν**. The cause of the service is not given.

443. **Λαομέδοντι**. Probably dat. of Advantage, § 21 (*a*).

446. **ἐγώ**. In vii 452 Apollo also builds.

πέρι. N.B. accent; cf. 57 (note).

448. **δ'**. For position see § 19.

εἰλίποδας ἕλικας, stock-epithets of βοῦς.

450. **πολυγηθέες**. Probably as bringing the glad changes of the year (Leaf).

451. Cf. Hor. *Od.* iii 3. 21 *Destituit deos mercede pacta Laomedon.*

454. **ἔπι** here probably = *to*, with gen. of Aim.

457. **μισθοῦ**, cf. note on αἰζηῶν (146).

458. **λαοῖσι**, i.e. Trojans; cf. 516.

μεθ' ἡμέων. A rare construction in Homer, § 23.

459. ὑπερφίαλοι, cf. 414.

461. ἐκάεργος. Stock-epithet; cf. 478.

462. Notice the sequence, οὐκ ἂν...μυθήσαιο...εἰ...πτολεμίξω.

464. Cf. vi 146 οἵη περ φύλλων γενεή, τοίη δὲ καὶ ἀνδρῶν.

467. μάχης, § 22 (c).

οἱ αὐτοί. Not *the same* but *they themselves.*

468. πάλιν ἐτράπετ', cf. 415.

475. μή...ἀκούσω (aor. subj.). A negative command in first person.

σευ. N.B. σέθεν in 331.

476. τὸ πρίν, *at that former time.*

478. τι. Adverbial accus., § 20 (b).

487. πολέμοιο, after δαήμεναι. For case see § 22 (e) and cf. *Od.* xi 174 εἰπὲ δέ μοι πατρός.

δαήμεναι. Either an infinitive of command (cf. 297) or we must understand after δαήμεναι some phrase =*fight* or *well and good.*

ὄφρ'...εἰδῆς. N.B. no ἂν, § 18 (d), but cf. 558.

488. ὅτι, cf. 411.

490. τόξα. Plural to denote bow + arrows; cf. 496, 502 and Verg. *Aen.* xii 350 *currus* (=chariot + horses).

492. ταχέες seems here more of an adverb than an adjective, cf. 37 (note).

494. ὑπ', *from under.*

πέτρην. Accus. of Motion to, § 23 (compound verbs).

496. ἡ, *she.*

497. διάκτορος Ἀργειφόντης. Stock-epithets.

498. δέ. For position cf. 448.

τι, cf. 478.

499. νεφεληγερέταο. Stock-epithet.

501. εὔχεσθαι. Infin. of Command, cf. 297.

κρατερῆφι βίηφιν, § 26.

504. θυγατέρος, probably goes with τόξα, but it might be the genit. of Aim after κίε, § 22 (e).

505. Nearly a repetition of 438.

506. γούνασι. Locative, § 21 (b). See also § 23 (compound verbs).

507. ἀμφί. Adverb.

προτὶ οἱ εἷλε, § 25. Notice ποτί (505), προτί (507), πρός (514).

508. **Κρονίδης**, though Κρονίων in 230, cf. Πηλείδης (251) and Πηλείων (327).

ἡδύ. Adverbial accus., § 20(*b*), cf. Hor. *Od.* i 22. 23 *dulce ridentem.*

510. Omitted in most MSS.

515. **ἐδύσετο.** Mixed aorist ; cf. note on ἴξον (1).

517. **ἤματι,** § 21 (*b*).

518. **οἱ,** *those.*

πρὸς Ὄλυμπον, though no preposition in 505.

519. **μέγα.** Adverbial accus., § 20 (*b*).

521. **μώνυχας ἵππους,** cf. 132.

522. **ὅτε...ἵκηται.** No ἄν, § 18 (*d*).

523. **θεῶν...ἀνῆκε.** A parenthesis. Notice the resemblance in the endings of these lines—ἀνῆκε, ἐφῆκεν, ἔθηκεν.

524. **πᾶσι.** Dat. of Disadvantage, § 21 (*a*), so too πολλοῖσι and Τρώεσσι (525).

526. **ὁ,** *that.*

θεῖου. As built by gods.

527. **ἐς** seems here to be separated from ἐνόησε by tmesis.

535. **ἐπανθέμεναι.** Infin. of command, cf. 297.

536. **ἄληται** is found only here. Leaf says we should expect ἄλεται as in ii 192.

538. **φάος.** Metaphorical.

539. **λοιγὸν ἀλάλκοι,** cf. 138.

540. **πόλιος,** though πόληος in 516.

541. Cf. Verg. *Georg.* iii 434 *asper siti.*

542. **ἔγχει.** For case see § 21 (*c*).

543. **κῦδος ἀρέσθαι,** cf. 596.

544. **υἷες Ἀχαιῶν,** cf. 376.

547. **ἐν,** § 25.

548. **κῆρας.** Another reading is χεῖρας.

549. **φηγῷ,** cf. 18 (note).

551. **πολλά.** Probably adverbial accus., § 20 (*b*).

552. A repetition of 53.

553. **ἅ μοι ἐγών.** A remarkable combination of cases. The dat. seems the true dat. (=*for*): the nomin. is perhaps the subject of some suppressed verb.

ὑπό, *from (under).*

554. τῇ, cf. 6 and ἄλλῃ (557).

οἱ, *those*, cf. 518.

The line bears some resemblance to 4.

556. The construction of the following lines is not quite clear, εἰ δ'... (556) seems parallel to εἰ δέ... (567) and as the latter has no apodosis it looks as though the former also has none—just as we often say in English *suppose this is the case..., suppose that....* Agenor supposes that (*a*) he flees to the city ; (*b*) he flees to the plain ; (*c*) he faces Achilles. The δ' in 560 looks like the δέ in apodosis (cf. 53), or we might perhaps express it in English by such a phrase as—*and then possibly in the evening I might make my way to the town* (for the sequence cf. 462). 562—566 give his reasons for rejecting the second supposition as useless.

559. κατά. Probably with ῥωπήια.

560. ἑσπέριος. Adverbial ; cf. ἐννύχιος (37 note).

ποταμοῖο. For case see § 22 (*d*).

561. ἱδρῶ. Perhaps an Adverbial accus. (§ 20 *b*) : the coolness was produced by the exudation of sweat. Some read ἱδρό' (dat.).

562. φίλος...θυμός, cf. φίλον ἦτορ (114).

563. μή depends on some verb of fearing understood, cf. 517.

564. με probably depends on μάρψῃ.

567. οἱ. Dat. of Disadvantage, § 21 (*a*).

568. τρωτός. The story of the invulnerability of Achilles seems to be post-Homeric.

574. τι, § 20 (*b*). For phrase cf. 288.

θυμῷ, § 21 (*b*).

576. εἰ περ...οὐτάσῃ. No ἄν, § 18 (*d*).

Notice different endings of οὐτάσῃ and βάλῃσιν, § 14 (*a*).

φθάμενος of course refers to the hunter.

577. ἀλλά. Used apparently with more freedom in early Greek than in Attic, cf. 276 : here it introduces the apodosis and = *yet still*.

περί, i.e. the spear was imbedded in the flesh.

578. ἀλκῆς, § 22 (*c*).

581. ἐΐσην = *round*.

582. αὐτοῖο, § 22 (*e*).

μέγ'. Adverbial accus., § 20 (*b*).

584. ἤματι, § 21 (*b*).

585. ἐπ' αὐτῇ, cf. 374 (note).

591. ὑπό, § 23 s.v.

592. μιν. Leaf reads οἱ.

593. σμερδαλέον. Adverbial accus., § 20 (b). For phrase cf. 255.
ἀπό. Adverb.

594. θεοῦ κ.τ.λ., cf. 165.

595. Ἀγήνορος. For case see § 22 (e).

596. δεύτερος. Adverbial ; cf. ἐννύχιος (37 note).

597. ἠέρι πολλῇ, cf. 549.

598. νέεσθαι. Epexegetic infin., § 18.

599. λαοῦ. Ablatival genitive, § 22 (c). See also § 23 (compound verbs).

600. πάντα. Adverbial accus., § 20 (b).

601. διώκειν. Epexegetic infin., § 18 (b).

602. πεδίοιο, cf. 247.
διώκετο. Notice middle, § 18 (a), though active in 601.

604. τυτθόν, § 20 (b).
ὑπεκπροθέοντα, § 24.

605. ὡς, final.

606. ὁμίλῳ, § 21 (c).

607. ἀσπάσιοι. Adverbial cf. ἐννύχιος (37 note).
ἀλέντων, § 22 (a).

609. ὅς seems here to be used in an indirect question ; cf. Arist. *Ach.* 118, ἐγῷδ' ὅς ἐστι. It is found elsewhere in Homer but usually when parallel to a previous ὅστις. We might perhaps translate—*to recognise the man—if any* (opt.)—*who had escaped and the man who had been slain* (indic.).

611. σαῶσαι, in agreement with γοῦνα. The optative expresses a kind of indefinite frequency.

VOCABULARY

The references are to the sections in the Introduction.

The meanings given are designedly simple. The student may often be able to think of some English term that will better suit the passage in which the word occurs.

ἀγαθός, probably originally denoted conduct or character of men of high birth, hence *good, brave, noble*; ἀγαθοῖο, gen. (§ 12).

ἀγακλεής, *famous.*

ἀγακλειτός, *famous.*

ἀγαυός, *noble.*

ἀγέρωχος, *lordly.*

ἄγη, *horror.*

'Αγήνωρ, Agenor, a Trojan.

ἀγήνωρ, *manly, proud.*

ἀγλαός, *fair, shining.*

ἀγξηράνῃ, aor. subj. of ἀναξηραίνω, *dry up* (§ 10 a).

ἀγορεύω, *speak, mention*; ἀγόρευον, impf.

ἄγριος, *fierce, savage.*

ἀγρότερος, *wild*; epithet of Artemis as huntress.

ἄγω, *lead, convey*; ἄγε, impf., also an exclamation, *come.*

ἀδδεές, perhaps voc. of ἀδεής, *fearless, shameless* (§ 8).

ἀεικής, *unseemly.*

ἀείρω, *raise.*

ἀέκων, *unwilling.*

ἄητο, impf. pass. of ἄημι, *blow.*

ἄητος, perhaps *flighty, stormy.*

ἀθάνατος, *undying.*

'Αθηναίη, 'Αθήνη, Athena, the goddess.

αἰ, see εἰ.

Αἰακίδης, Aeacides, i.e. Achilles, grandson of Aeacus; Αἰακίδαο, gen. (§ 12).

Αἰακός, *Aeacus.*

αἰγίοχος, *aegis-wearing*; αἰγιόχοιο, gen. (§ 12).

αἰγίς, aegis, part of the equipment of Zeus, but often used by Athena and on at least one occasion by Apollo. It seems to have been a kind of λαισήιον, i.e. the skin of some animal suspended from the left shoulder and extended by the left hand as a kind of shield. The story of the Gorgon's head on it is post-Homeric. (Leaf suggests that the fringe may have been thought to resemble snakes.) The word has been connected with αἴξ, *goat* — probably wrongly—and ἀίσσω, *rush*, as being worn by Athena when she rushed against the giants (Bayfield). It has been suggested also that it may be connected with the root of the English word *oak* and so may have originally denoted a wooden shield.

ἀιδήλως, *destructively.*

'Αίδης, *Hades*—in Homer almost always the god and not his realm; 'Αίδαο, gen. (§ 12).

αἰδοῖος, *deserving of respect*;

αἰδοίοιο, gen.; αἰδοίης, dat. pl. fem. (§ 12).

αἴδομαι, respect, be ashamed; αἴδετο, impf.; αἴδεο, pres. imper.

αἰεί, αἰέν, always.

αἰετός, eagle.

αἰζηός, vigorous, hence warrior.

αἴθω, kindle; αἰθομένοιο, gen. pres. part. pass. (§ 12).

αἷμα, blood.

Αἴνιος, Aenius, a Trojan.

αἴνυμαι, take; αἴνυτο, impf.

αἰπήεις, high.

αἰπός, high, sheer; as applied to streams it may refer to rapids or to the steepness of their banks, or like Latin altus may =deep as well as high.

αἱρέω, take; in middle choose; ᾕρεε, impf.; εἷλες, ἕλον, aor. ind. act.; ἑλών, aor. part. act.; εἵλετο, aor. ind. mid.; ἕληται, aor. subj. mid.

αἴσιμος, fated.

ἀίσσω, rush; ἤιξεν, aor.

αἴσυλος, evil; perhaps from ἀρισος=iniquus (Leaf).

αἰσχρός, shameful; αἴσχιον, compar.

αἴτιος, responsible.

αἶψα, forthwith, quickly.

ἀίω, hear; ἀίε, impf.

ἀκάματος, tireless.

ἀκαχμένος, sharpened.

Ἀκεσσαμενός, Acessamenus; Ἀκεσσαμενοῖο, gen. (§ 12).

ἀκηδής, heedless, or without due rites of mourning.

ἀκήριος, spiritless.

ἀκούω, hear; ἄκουσε(ν), aor. ind.; ἀκούσω, aor. subj.

ἀκρίς, locust.

ἀκροκελαινιόων, part. of ἀκροκελαινιάω, grow black on the surface (§ 10 i).

ἀκτή, corn, meal.

ἀκωκή, point, edge.

ἄκων, dart.

ἀλαλητός, cry.

ἀλάλκοι, ward off, aor. opt. (no present) (§ 13 d).

ἄλγος, grief, pain.

ἀλείς, see εἴλω.

ἀλέξω, ward off; ἀλεξήσω, fut.

ἄληται, see ἅλλομαι.

ἀλιμυρήεις, flowing into sea, or flowing with brine.

ἅλις, in heaps, in crowds.

ἀλκή, might, help.

ἄλκιμος, brave.

ἀλλά, but (see however notes on 276 and 577).

ἀλλέξαι=ἀναλέξαι (§ 10 a), aor. inf. of ἀναλέγω, collect.

ἀλλήλους, one another.

ἅλλομαι, leap; ἆλτο, aor. ind. (§ 13 c); ἄληται, aor. subj.

ἄλλος, other; ἄλλῃ, by another way (§ 21 b).

ἄλλοτε, at one time, at another time.

ἄλλυδις, in different directions.

ἄλοχος, spouse, wife.

ἅλς, sea; ἁλός, gen.; ἁλόθεν, see § 26.

Ἅλτης, Altes; Ἄλταο and Ἄλτεω, gen. (§ 12).

ἆλτο, see ἅλλομαι.

ἀλύσκω, escape; ἀλύξαι, aor. inf.

ἀλωή, threshing floor, garden, orchard.

ἀλώμεναι=ἀλῶναι, inf. of ἑάλων (ἐϝαλων), aor. of ἁλίσκομαι, be taken (§ 15 b).

ἄμ, see ἀνά (§ 10 a).

ἅμα, at the same time.

ἀμάρα, trench.

ἀμαρτῆ, at the same time, at once; see note on 162.

ἀμαχητί, without fighting.

ἀμβολάδην, bubbling up (adv.) (§ 10 a).

ἀμβρόσιος, an adjective of doubtful origin and meaning. Some connect it with a Semitic word meaning *perfume* and translate it *fragrant*. Others derive it from ἀ, *not* + μβροτός, *mortal*, and translate it *divine*. Possibly two different words have been confused.

ἀμείλικτος, *harsh*.

ἀμείνων, *better*.

ἄμεναι, see ἄω.

ἄμμες, see ἐγώ.

ἀμύμων, originally *blameless*, but in Homer little more than a conventional epithet = *noble, excellent*.

ἀμύνω, *help* (with dat.).

ἀμφαραβέω, *clang around*.

ἀμφί, see § 23.

ἀμφιπένομαι, *be busied about* (especially of tending a wounded man).

ἀμφίς, see § 23.

ἀμφότερος, ἄμφω, *both*.

ἄν, see § 18 *d*.

ἀνά, see § 23.

ἄναλκις, *helpless, coward*.

ἄναξ, *lord*.

ἀναπνέω, *breathe again, get a respite*; ἀναπνεύσωσιν, aor. subj.

ἀνάσσω, *rule* (with dat.).

ἀναστήσονται, see ἀνίσταμαι.

ἀναχασσάμενος, aor. part. of ἀναχάζομαι, *recoil*.

ἀνδρόμεος, *human*; ἀνδρομέοιο, gen. (§ 12).

ἀνεμώλιος, *vain*.

ἀνέρομαι, *ask*; ἀνείρετο, impf.

ἄνεσαν, see ἀνίημι.

ἀνέσχετο, aor. ind. mid. of ἀνέχω, see § 23.

ἄνευθεν, see § 23.

ἀνῆκας, ἀνῆκεν, see ἀνίημι.

ἀνήρ, *man*; ἀνέρος, gen.; ἀνέρι, dat.; ἄνδρεσσιν, dat. pl. (§ 12).

ἄνθρωπος, *man*.

ἀνιάζω, *grieve*.

ἀνίημι, *excite, loose*; ἀνῆκα, aor. (ἄνεσαν, 3rd pl.).

ἀνίσταμαι, *rise*; ἀναστήσονται, fut.

ἀνορούω, *start up*.

ἄνοος, *foolish*.

ἄντα, see § 23.

Ἀντήνωρ, *Antenor*, a Trojan.

ἀντί, see § 23.

ἀντιάω, *meet* (dat.); ἀντιόωσιν, pres. ind. (§ 10 *i*); ἀντιόωσα, pres. part. (§ 10 *i*).

ἀντιβίην, *face to face* (advb.).

ἀντίθεος, *equal to the gods*.

ἀντίος, *opposing*.

ἀντιφερίζω, ἀντιφέρομαι, *match* (with acc. and dat.).

ἄντυξ, *rim*.

ἀνώιστος, *unthought of, unlooked for*.

ἆξαι, inf. of ἔαξα, aor. of ἄγνυμι, *break*.

Ἀξιός, *Axius*, a river in Macedon.

ἄορ, *sword*.

ἀπαείρομαι, *depart*.

ἀπαίσσω, *spring from* (with gen.); ἀπαΐξας, aor. part.

ἀπαλοτρεφής, *plump*.

ἀπαμείβομαι, *answer*.

ἅπας, *all*.

ἀπαυράω, *take away*; ἀπηύρα, impf.; ἀπούρας (=ἀπο-υρας or ἀπορρας), aor. part.

ἀπειλέω, *threaten*; ἠπείλησε, aor.

ἀπεχθάνομαι, *be hated*; ἀπηχθόμην, aor. (ἀπεχθέσθαι, inf.).

ἀπηύρα, see ἀπαυράω.

ἀπό, see § 23.

ἀποβαίνω, *go away*; ἀπεβήτην, aor. ind. 3rd dual.

ἀποέργαθον, aor. of ἀπείργω, *ward off* (§ 13 *e*).

ἀποέρσῃ, aor. subj. of probably ἀπορερρω (cf. Lat. *verro*), *sweep away*; ἀποέρσειε, opt.

ἄποινα (neut. pl.), *recompense, ransom*.

ἀπολεψέμεν, fut. inf. of ἀπολέπω, *lop off* (§ 15 *b*).

ἀπολήγω, *cease* (with gen.).

ἀπολιχμάομαι, *lick off.*

ἀπόλλυμι, *destroy,* in middle *perish;* ἀπόλωνται, aor. subj. mid.

Ἀπόλλων, *Apollo,* the god.

ἀπονέομαι, *depart.*

ἀποπαύω, *stop.*

ἀποπέμπω, *send away.*

ἀπορούω, *dart away.*

ἀποτίνω, *atone for, pay;* ἀποτισέμεν, fut. inf. (§ 15 *b*).

ἀποτρέπω, *turn away.*

ἀπούρας, see ἀπαυράω.

ἀποψυχθείς, aor. part. pass. of ἀποψύχω, *cool.*

ἀπῶσαν, aor. of ἀπωθέω, *thrust back.*

ἄρ, ἄρα, see § 5 and 10 *a*.

ἀραρυίας, pf. part. of ἀραρίσκω, *fit.*

ἀργαλέος, *grievous.*

Ἀργεῖος, *Argive.* (In Homer Argos denotes the Peloponnese rather than the town, "Pelasgian Argos" = Thessaly.)

Ἀργειφόντης, a common epithet of Hermes; used to be derived from Ἄργος and φονεύω and so = *slayer of Argus,* but this legend seems not to be known to Homer, and the word is probably connected with ἀργός (= *white* and so *gleaming*) and φαίνομαι and so means *swift-appearing.*

ἀργεστής, *white;* ἀργεστᾶο, gen. (§ 12). As applied to Νότος the word may refer to the wind clearing the sky or bringing white clouds, cf. *albus Notus* (Hor.).

ἀργέτα, acc. of ἀργής, *white, shining* (§ 10 *c*).

ἀργυροδίνης, *with silvery eddies.*

ἀργυρότοξος, *with silver bow.*

ἀρειή, *threat.*

ἀρείων, *mightier.*

ἀρέσθαι, inf. of ἠρόμην, aor. mid. of αἴρω, *raise;* in middle *win.*

ἀρήιος, *warlike.*

Ἄρης, *Ares,* the war-god, *battle;* Ἄρηα, acc.; Ἄρει, dat.

Ἀρίσβη, *Arisbe,* a place in the Troad on the Hellespont.

ἄριστος, *best, bravest.*

ἀρκέω, *defend, help* (with dat.); ἀρκέσει, fut. (§ 10 *c*).

ἅρμα, *chariot.*

ἄρουρα, *arable land, ground.*

ἄρρηκτος, *inviolable.*

Ἄρτεμις, *Artemis,* the goddess.

ἄρχω, *begin* (with gen.).

ἀρωγή, ἀρωγός, *help.*

ἆσαι, see ἄω.

ἀσθμαίνω, *gasp.*

ἄσις, *mud.*

ἀσπάσιος, *glad.*

ἀσπίς, *shield.*

Ἀστεροπαῖος, *Asteropaeus,* a Trojan.

ἄστυ, *city.*

Ἀστύπυλος, *Astypylus,* a Trojan.

ἀτάρ, *but.*

ἄτερ, see § 23.

ἀτρυτώνη, epithet applied to Athena; perhaps means *tameless* or *unwearied,* but the origin of the word is doubtful. It may have something to do with the words *Triton, Amphitrite;* Τριτογένεια, which the Greeks connected with the lake Tritonis in Libya, or the river Triton in N. Greece.

ἀτυζόμενος, *terrified.*

αὖ, αὖτε, *again, but.*

αὐδάω, *say;* ηὔδα, impf.

αὐτάρ, *but* (without much idea of contrast).

ἀυτέω, *cry;* ἀύτει, impf.

αὐτίκα, *forthwith.*

αὖτις, *again, back.*

ἀυτμή, *breath.*

αὐτόθι, *there, on the spot* (§ 26).

VOCABULARY

43

αὐτός, *self;* in oblique cases *him,* etc.

αὐτοῦ, *there.*

αὕτως, *in the very way, thus.*

αὐχήν, *neck.*

ἀύω, *call;* ἄυσε, aor.

ἀφάμαρτεν, aor. of ἀφαμαρτάνω, *miss* (with gen.).

ἄφαρ, *straightway.*

ἀφίημι, *fling away, hurl, send;* ἀφ(έ)ηκεν, aor.

ἀφίσταμαι, *stand aloof;* ἀφέστασαν, plup.

'Αφροδίτη, *Aphrodite,* goddess of love.

ἀφρός, *foam.*

'Αχαιός, *Achaean,* usual term for Greek.

'Αχελώιος, *Achelous,* river in W. Greece.

'Αχιλεύς, 'Αχιλλεύς, *Achilles;* 'Αχιλῆος, gen.

ἄψ, *back.*

ἅψασθαι, aor. inf. of ἅπτομαι, *touch* (with gen.).

ἄψορρος, *returning, going back.*

ἄω, *take one's fill of* (gen.); ἄμεναι, pres. inf. (§ 15 *b*); ἆσαι, aor. inf.

βαθυδινήεις, βαθυδίνης, *deep-eddying.*

βαθυρρείτης, *deep-flowing;* βαθυρρείταο, gen. (§ 12).

βαθύρροος, *deep-flowing.*

βαθύς, *deep, dense;* βαθέης, βαθείης, gen. sing. fem.; βαθείησιν, dat. pl. fem. (§ 12).

βαίνω, *go;* βαῖνε, impf.; βῆ, aor.

βάλλω, *throw, strike;* in middle *consider;* βάλε(ν), βάλες, aor. ind.; βάλησιν, aor. subj. (§ 14); βάλλεο, pres. imper. mid.; βλημένου, aor. part. pass. (§ 13 *c*).

βαρύς, *heavy.*

βεβριθυῖα, *grievous;* pf. part. of βρίθω, *be heavy.*

βέλος, *missile, dart;* βελέεσσιν, dat. pl. (§ 12).

βέλτερος, *better.*

βῆ, see βαίνω.

βίη, *force;* βίης, gen.; βίηφι, *by force* (§ 26).

βιήσατο, aor. mid. of βιάω, *force, rob* (double acc.).

βλημένου, see βάλλω.

Βορέης, *Boreas, north-wind.*

βουκολέεσκες, past tense of βουκολέω, *tend cattle* (§ 13 *a*).

βουλή, *plan, counsel.*

βοῦς, *ox.*

βράχε, aor. or impf. of βράχω (?), *clash, resound.*

βροντή, *thunder.*

βροτολοιγός, *bane of men.*

βροτός, *mortal.*

γάρ, *for* (§ 5).

γαίη, *earth;* γαίῃ, dat.

γαστήρ, *belly.*

γέ, see § 5.

γείνομαι, *be born;* γείνασθαι, γείνατο, aor. (in transitive sense = *beget, bring forth*).

γελάω, *laugh;* (ἐ)γέλασσε, aor. (§ 8).

γενεή, *race, family;* γενεῆφι (§ 26).

γενόμην, γενόμεσθα, see γίγνομαι.

γένος, *race.*

γέρων, *aged.*

γεύομαι, *taste* (with gen.); γεύσεται, fut. ind. or aor. subj. (§ 15 *a*).

γεφυρόω, *bridge, dam.*

γῆ, *earth.*

γηθοσύνη, *joy.*

γίγνομαι, *become, be born;* γίγνετ', impf.; γενόμην, γενόμεσθα, aor.

γνώμεναι, aor. inf. of γίγνωσκω, *ascertain* (§ 15 *b*).

γοάω, *bewail.*

γόνυ, *knee;* γοῦνα (= γονϝα), γούνατα, acc. pl.; γούνων, gen. pl.; γούνασι, dat. pl.

γουνόομαι, *implore.*

γυῖον, *limb.*

γυμνός, *without full clothing or armour.*

γυνή, *woman.*

δαείω, subj. (§ 15) of ἐδάην (aor., no pres.), *learn;* δαήμεναι, inf. (§ 15 b).

δαίζω, *cleave, slay;* δαϊζέμεναι, inf. (§ 15 b).

δαικτάμενος, *slain;* possibly should be written δαὶ κτάμενος (from κτείνω) = *slain in battle.*

δαίμων, *god.*

δαίω, *kindle, burn;* δαίετο, impf.; δάηται, aor. subj.

δακρύεις, *weeping.*

δαμάζω, δαμάω, δαμνάω, δάμνημι, *subdue;* δάμνησι, pres. ind.; ἐδάμνα, impf.; δάμασσας, aor. part. (§ 8); δαμάσσεται, aor. subj. mid. (§ 15 a); δάμη, aor. ind. pass. of which δαμῆναι and δαμήμεναι (§ 15 b) are inf. and δαμέντα part.

δάπτω, *rend, devour.*

Δαρδανίδης, *son of Dardanus,* founder of Troy; Δαρδανίδαο, gen. (§ 12).

δέ, *and, but.* See note on 53.

δείδια (= δέδϝια), perf. (with a pres. sense) of perhaps δείδω, *fear,* whence δείσας, aor. part.

δείελος, *evening;* perhaps *evening star* or *setting sun* (Leaf).

δείλη, *afternoon.*

δεινός, *dread, terrible;* δεινοῖο, gen. (§ 12).

δειροτομέω, *cut the throat.*

δείσας, see δείδια.

δελφίς, *dolphin.*

δέμας, *form, body.*

δένδρεον, *tree.*

δεξιτερός, *right;* in fem. *right hand.*

δεύτερος, *second;* often = adv. *next* (§ 23).

δεύω, *wet;* δεῦε, impf.

δέω, *bind;* δήσει, fut.; δῆσε, aor.

δή, see § 5.

δηθά, *long.*

δήϊος, *hostile.*

Δημήτηρ, *Demeter,* goddess of corn.

δημός, *fat.*

δηριάομαι, *contend;* δηριαάσθων, pres. imper. (§ 10 i).

δηρόν, *long.*

δῆσε, δήσειν, see δέω.

διά, see § 23.

διαίνω, *wet;* δίαινε, impf.

διάκτορος (probably connected with διώκω), *runner;* epithet of Hermes.

διαλέγομαι, *converse.*

διαπρό, *right through* (§ 24).

διατμήξας, aor. part. of διατμήγω, *cut in twain.*

δίδωμι, *give;* δῶκε, ἔδωκεν, aor.

διέσταμεν, 1st pl. perf. (in pres. sense) with intrans. meaning, *stand apart;* from διίστημι.

Διί, Διός, see Ζεύς.

διιπετής, *fallen from heaven;* see note on 2.

δίνη, *eddy;* δίνῃσι, dat. pl. (§ 12).

δινήεις, *eddying, whirling.*

διογενής, *high-born, noble;* a conventional epithet of kings and princes.

Διομήδης, *Diomede,* the Greek warrior.

δῖος, *bright, illustrious;* often a mere conventional epithet.

διοτρεφής, *nurtured from heaven;* as applied to rivers see note on 2.

δίχα, *in two ways.*

δίψη, *thirst.*

διώκω, *pursue;* διώκετο, impf. mid.

δίωσεν, aor. of διωθέω, *push away.*

δολιχεγχής, *with long spear.*

δολιχόσκιος, *long-shafted* (δολιχο-σχ-ιος, conn. with ἔσχον) or *casting a long shadow* (δολιχο-σκια).

δόλος, *craft*.

δόρυ, *spear*; δουρός (=δορϝος), gen.; δουρί, dat.; δοῦρε, dual; δούρασιν, dat. pl.

δουρικλυτός, *famed with the spear*.

δύναμαι, *be able*; δύνατ’, 3rd sing. impf.

δύστηνος, *unhappy*.

δύω, (adj.) *two*; (vb.) *sink* or *enter*; δῦ, aor. act.; ἐδύσετο, aor. mid. (§ 13 *b*).

δυώδεκα, *twelve*.

δυωδέκατος, *twelfth*.

δῶ, δῶμα, *house*.

δῶκε, see δίδωμι.

δῶρον, *gift*.

ἑ, *him* (see note on 64); σφίν, dat. pl.

ἑανός, *robe*.

ἐάω, *allow, leave*; ἔασεν, aor. *whence*; ἔασον, imper.; ἐάσω, subj.

ἐγγύς, *near*.

ἐγέλασσε, see γελάω.

ἔγχελυς, *eel*.

ἔγχος, ἐγχείη, *lance*.

ἐγώ(ν), *I*; ἐμεῦ, μευ (§ 10 *g*), ἐμεῖο, ἐμέθεν (§ 26), gen.; ἡμέων, gen. pl.; ἄμμες, nom. pl.; νῶϊ, dual.

ἐδάμνα, see δαμάζω.

ἔδειμα, aor. of δέμω, *build*.

ἐδύσετο, see δύω.

ἔδω, *eat*.

ἔδωκεν, see δίδωμι.

ἐέλσαι, see εἴλω.

ἕζομαι, *sit*; ἕζετο, impf. or aor.

ἔθανε, see θνῄσκω.

ἐθείρῃ, pres. subj. of ἐθείρω, *tend* (?).

ἐθέλω, *be willing*; ἔθελε(ν), ἤθελε, impf.; ἐθέλησθα, 2nd sing. pres. subj. (§ 14).

ἔθηκεν, see τίθημι.

εἰ, *if*.

εἴδῃς, see οἶδα.

εἶδον, see ὁράω.

εἶδος, *form, shape*.

εἶεν, see εἰμί.

εἴκτην, εἰκώς, see ἔοικα.

εἶλες, εἷλετο, see αἱρέω.

εἰλέω, *force together*; εἰλεῦντο, impf. (§ 10 *g*).

εἰλήλουθα, see ἔρχομαι.

εἰλίπους, *shambling*, used of oxen as swinging their feet round when walking.

εἰλύω, *cover*.

εἴλω, *gather together*; ἔλσαι, ἐέλσαι, aor. inf.; from an aor. pass. ἐάλην comes part. ἀλείς.

εἵμαρτο (? =ἐσέσμαρτο), *it was fated*; plup. of μείρομαι, *receive as one’s lot*.

εἰμέν, see εἰμί.

εἰμί, *be, be able*; εἶς (? ἐσσί), 2nd sing. pres. ind.; εἰμέν, 1st pl. pres. ind.; ἔμ(μ)εναι, pres. inf. (§ 15 *b*); ἐών, pres. part.; ἦεν, 3rd sing. impf.; ἔσαν, 3rd pl. impf.; ἔσσεται, ἔσται, fut. ind.

εἶμι, *will go*; to the pres. tense belong εἶσι, 3rd sing. ind.; ἴομεν (§ 15 *a*), subj.; ἴμεν (§ 15 *b*), ἰέναι, inf.; ἰών, part.; to the past tense ἴσαν, 3rd pl. ind.

εἷος, *while*.

εἶπον, aor. of λέγω, *say*.

εἰρύομεσθα, εἰρύσαο, see ἐρύω.

εἷς, see εἰμί and note on 150.

εἰς, ἐς, see § 23.

εἰσάμενος, aor. part. of εἴδομαι, *be like to*.

εἴσεαι, see οἶδα.

εἰσέπτατο, aor. of εἰσπέτομαι, *fly into*.

ἐΐσκω, *liken, deem*; ἠΐσκομεν, impf.

εἰς ὅ κε, *until*.

εἴσομαι, see ἵημι.

εἶσος, see ἴσος.

εἴσω, see § 23.

εἶχε, see ἔχω.

ἐκ, ἐξ, see § 23.

ἐκάεργος, *far-working* (i.e. *shooting*) or *keeper afar* (of pestilence); epithet of Apollo.

ἑκατόμβοιος, *value of* 100 *oxen.*

ἔκβαλλε, impf. of ἐκβάλλω, *fling out.*

ἐκγεγαῶτι, dat. of pf. part. of ἐκγίγνομαι, *spring from.*

ἔκπαγλος, *dread.*

ἐκπέμπω, *send out.*

ἐκπέρσαντες, aor. part.; ἐκπέρσει, fut. of ἐκπέρθω, *sack utterly.*

ἔκπιπτον, impf. of ἐκπίπτω, *fall out.*

ἐκτός, see § 23.

Ἕκτωρ, *Hector*, son of Priam king of Troy.

ἐκφέρω, *bring about.*

ἐκφυγέειν, aor. inf. of ἐκφεύγω, *escape.*

ἐκχύμενος, aor. part. mid. of ἐκχέω, *pour out* (§ 13 c).

ἐλαύνω, *drive;* ἤλασε, aor. (ἐλάσας part.).

ἔλαφος, *deer.*

ἕλε, ἕλον, see αἱρέω.

ἐλεαίρω, *pity;* ἐλέαιρεν, impf.

ἐλεεινός, *piteous.*

ἐλέησον, aor. imper. of ἐλεέω, *pity.*

ἐλεύσεται, see ἔρχομαι.

ἕληται, see αἱρέω.

ἐλθών, see ἔρχομαι.

ἕλιξ, perhaps *with twisted horns.*

ἑλίσσω, *roll.*

ἐλλίσσετο, impf. of λίσσομαι, *pray* (§ 8).

ἕλπω, *make to hope;* ἔολπα (= ϝεϝολπα), intrans. pf.

ἕλσαι, see εἴλω.

ἐμβάλλω, *cast into* (with dat. § 25); ἔμβαλεν, aor.

ἐμέ, ἐμέθεν, ἐμεῖο, ἐμοί, ἐμεῦ, see ἐγώ.

ἔμ(μ)εναι, see εἰμί.

ἐμός, *my;* ἐμῇσ' dat. pl. fem. (§ 12).

ἐμπίπλημι, *fill;* ἐμπίπληθι, pres. imper. (§ 14); ἔμπληντο, aor. (§ 13 c).

ἐν, ἐνί, see § 23.

ἐναίρω, *slay.*

ἐναντίβιον, *face to face* (adv.).

ἐναντίον, see § 23.

ἐναρίζω, *strip of arms, spoil.*

ἔναυλος, *torrent.*

ἕνδεκα, *eleven.*

ἑνδέκατος, *eleventh.*

ἔνδον, *within.*

ἕνεκα, see § 23.

ἐνεστήρικτο, plup. pass. of ἐνστηρίζω, *fix in.*

ἐνηής, *kind, gentle.*

ἔνθα, ἐνθάδε, *here, there, then.*

ἐνθεμένη, aor. part. mid. of ἐντίθημι, *place in.*

ἔνθεν, *hence, thence, whence.*

ἐνιαυτός, *year.*

ἔννεον, impf. of ἐννέω, *swim in:* but see note on 11.

ἐννοσίγαιος, ἐνοσίχθων, *earth-shaker:* epithets of Poseidon as lord of the earthquake or owing to the beating of waves on the shore.

ἐννύχιος, *by night* (adj.), see note on 37.

ἐνταυθοῖ, *there.*

ἐντροπαλιζόμενος, *oft turning round.*

ἐνωπῇ, *openly.*

ἐξαίφνης, *suddenly.*

ἐξαποτίνω, *satisfy.*

ἐξαρπάζω, *snatch away;* ἐξήρπαξε, aor.

ἐξέθορε, aor. of ἐκθρώσκω, *leap out.*

ἐξελάσειε, aor. opt. of ἐξελαύνω, *drive out.*

ἐξεναρίζω, *strip of arms.*

ἐξῆγε, impf. of ἐξάγω, *lead out.*

ἐξηράνθη, aor. pass. of ξηραίνω, *dry up.*

ἔοικα, *be like* (with dat.), *seem,*

be seemly; pf. in pres. sense of
ϝείκω (?); εἰκώς, part.; ἔϊκτην,
dual plup.

ἔολπα, see ἔλπω.

ἔοργα (= ϝεϝοργα, cf. τέτροφα
from τρέπω), pf. of ἔρδω, *do.*

ἐπαινέω, *praise;* ἐπαινήσαντος,
aor. part.

ἐπαμύνω, *help.*

ἐπᾶλτο, aor. of ἐφάλλομαι, *spring on* (§ 13 *c*).

ἐπανθέμεναι, aor. inf. of ἐπανα-
τίθημι, *put to* (§ 15 *b*).

ἐπεί, *when.*

ἐπείγω, *impel.*

ἔπειτα, *then.*

ἐπέλασσε, aor. of πελάζω, *bring near* (§ 8).

ἐπέρασσα, ἐπέρησε, see περάω.

ἔπεσον, see πίπτω.

ἐπέσσυτο, aor. (§ 13 *c*) of ἐπι-
σεύομαι, *hasten to, rush on* (with dat.).

ἔπετο, see ἕπομαι.

ἐπεύχομαι, *vaunt over* (with dat.).

ἔπεφνον, aor. of φένω, *slay.*

ἐπέφρασω, 2nd sing. aor. ind.
mid. of ἐπιφράζομαι, *observe.*

ἐπέχω, *lie upon, cover;* ἐπέσχε, aor.

ἐπί, see § 23. ἔπι=ἔπεστι, *is on.*

ἐπιγνάμψας, aor. part. of ἐπι-
γνάμπτω, *curve, bend.*

ἐπιγράβδην, *grazingly.*

ἐπιεισαμένη, aor. part. mid. of
ἔπειμι, *approach.*

ἐπίκουρος, *helper.*

ἐπιμίξ, *confusedly.*

ἐπινεφρίδιος, *on the kidneys.*

ἐπισπεῖν, see ἐφέπω.

ἐπίσταμαι, *know;* ἐπιστήσονται, fut.

ἐπιστροφάδην, *turning this way
and that* (adv.).

ἐπιστώσαντο, aor. mid. of πισ-
τόω, *bind by oath, pledge.*

ἐπιτάρροθος, perhaps = ἐπίρρο-

θος, lit. *coming up with shouts,*
i.e. *helper.*

ἐπιτέλλω, *ordain.*

ἐπιτρέπω, *give, yield.*

ἔπομαι, *follow;* ἕπετο, impf.

ἐποροúω, *rush upon* (with dat.).

ἔπος, *word, speech;* ἔπεα, acc.
pl.; ἐπέεσσιν, dat. pl. (§ 12).

ἐπτά, *seven.*

ἐπῶρτο, aor. mid. of ἐπόρνυμαι,
rush on (§ 13 *c*).

ἐρατεινός, *lovely.*

ἔργον, *deed.*

ἐρεείνω, *ask.*

ἔρεξε, see ῥέζω.

ἐρέπτομαι, *feed on.*

ἐρέω, fut. of λέγω, *say.*

ἐρίβωλος, *fertile.*

ἐριζέμεναι, pres. inf. (§ 15) of
ἐρίζω, *strive* (with dat.).

ἐρινεός, *wild fig.*

ἐρινύες, *curses:* properly the
ancient deities who were
thought to punish crimes,
especially against parents.

ἐριποῦσα, aor. part. of ἐρείπω,
fall (§ 13 *c*).

ἔρις, *strife.*

ἐρισθενής, *very mighty.*

ἐρυθαίνετο, impf. pass. of ἐρυ-
θαίνω, *redden.*

ἐρύκω, *check;* ἐρυκέμεν, inf.
(§ 15 *b*); ἐρύκακε, ἠρύκακε, aor.
(§ 13 *d*).

ἐρύω (= ϝερύω), *draw;* ἐρύσσαι,
aor. inf.; in middle (if this is
the same verb), *protect, keep;*
εἰρύμεσθα, impf.; ἐρύσσεσθαι,
fut. inf.; εἰρύσαο (§ 14), 2nd
sing. aor. ind. mid. (ἐρυσσάμενος, part.).

ἐρχθέντα, aor. part. pass. of
εἴργω, *shut in.*

ἔρχομαι, *come, go;* ἐλεύσεται,
fut.; ἤλυθε, ἦλθε, aor. (ἐλθών,
part.); εἰλήλουθα, pf.

ἐρωή, *rush, throw* (noun).

ἔς, see εἰς.

ἐσαγείρομαι, *collect;* ἐσαγείρετο, impf.

ἔσαν, see εἰμί.

ἔσεσθαι, see εἰμί.

ἐσέχυντο, aor. mid. of ἐσχέω, *pour in* (§ 13 c).

ἐσθίω, *eat;* φάγῃσι, 3rd sing. aor. subj. (§ 14).

ἔσθορε, aor. of ἐσθρώσκω, *leap in.*

ἑσπέριος, *in the evening.* See note on 37.

ἔσσεται, ἔσται, see εἰμί.

ἐσσυμένως, *hastily.*

ἔστη, ἐστήκει, see ἴστημι.

ἔσχεν, ἔσχετο, see ἔχω.

ἑταῖρος (=ἕταρος?), *comrade.*

ἐτέλεσσεν, aor. of τελέω, *pay* (§ 8).

ἕτερος, *the one, the other;* in fem. sc. *hand.*

ἔτι, *still, any longer.*

ἔτλαν, 3rd pl. of ἔτλην, aor. (§ 14) of τλάω, *dare, undertake;* ἔτλης, 2nd sing.

ἐτράπετο, see τρέπω.

ἔτραφε, intrans. aor. of τρέφω, *nourish.*

ἐύ, *well.*

ἐύδμητος, *well-built;* ἐϋδμήτοιο, gen. (§ 12).

ἐυκτίμενος, *well-built.*

ἐύορμος, *with good moorings.*

ἐυρρεῖος = ἐυρρεῖος, gen. of ἐυρρεής, *fair-flowing.*

ἐύρροος, *fair-flowing.*

εὐρυρέεθρος, *broad-flowing.*

εὐρύς, *broad, wide.*

ἐυστέφανος, *fair-garlanded* or *well-girdled.*

ἐύτμητος, *well-cut.*

ἐυφυής, *well-grown, goodly.*

εὔχομαι, *pray, vow, vaunt.*

εὖχος, *petition* (i.e. thing prayed for).

ἔφαθ' (ἔφατο), see φημί.

ἐφέζετο, impf. of ἐφέζομαι, *sit at.*

ἐφέπω, *follow, meet;* ἔφεπ', impf.; ἐπισπεῖν, aor. inf.

ἐφετμή, *behest, command.*

ἔφη, see φημί.

ἐφῆκε(ν), aor. of ἐφίημι, *send upon, hurl at.*

ἐφῆπται, 3rd sing. pf. pass. of ἐφάπτω, *fasten on* (with dat.).

ἔχμα, *obstacle.*

ἔχραε, 3rd sing. aor. of root χραυ- or χραϝ=*touch,* hence *attack* and so *wish* (Leaf).

ἔχω (=σεχω), *have, hold, check, be able;* ἔχε(ν), εἶχε, impf.; ἔσχεν, aor. (σχῶμεν, subj.; σχεῖν, inf.; ἔσχετο, σχέτο, ind. mid.; σχέο, imper. mid.).

ἔων, see εἰμί.

ζαφλεγής, *fiery.*

Ζεύς, *Zeus;* Διός, Ζηνός, gen.; Διί, dat.

Ζέφυρος, *north-west wind;* Ζεφύροιο, gen. (§ 12).

ζέω, *boil;* ζέε, impf.

ζόφος, *gloom,* especially of lower world.

ζωός, *alive.*

ἡ, see ὁ.

ἦ (vb.), 3rd sing. of impf. or aor. of ἠμί, *say* (retained in Attic in phrase ἦ δ' ὅς, *said he*); (particle), see § 5.

ᾗ, *where,* from ὅς (cf. Lat. *qua*).

ἠγάθεος, *most holy.*

ἦγε, see ἄγω.

ἡγεμονεύω, *guide.*

ἥδε, see ὅδε.

ἠδέ, *and* (§ 5).

ἡδύς, *pleasant.*

ἦεν, see εἰμί.

ἠερέθομαι, *flutter.*

ἠερόεις, *misty.*

Ἠετίων, *Eetion,* an Imbrian.

ἠήρ, *mist;* ἠέρα, acc.; ἠέρι, dat.

ἤιξε, see ἀίσσω.

ἠίσκομεν, see ἴσκω.

ἧκε, see ἵημι.

ἤλασε, see ἐλαύνω.

ἦλθε, ἤλυθε, see ἔρχομαι.
ἦλφον, aor. ind. of ἀλφάνω, *earn.*
ἦμαρ, *day;* ἤματι, dat.
ἤμενος, part. of ἧμαι, *sit.*
ἡμέτερος, *our;* ἡμετέροιο, gen. (§ 12).
ἡμέων, see ἐγώ.
ἥμισυς, *half.*
ἠπείλησε, see ἀπειλέω.
ἦρεε, see αἱρέω.
Ἥρη, *Hera,* wife of Zeus.
ἦρχε, see ἄρχω.
ἥρως, *hero.*
ἡσύχιος, *quiet.*
ἦτορ, *heart.* (Leaf says it = *animus* and was used primarily of vitality and then—and usually —of passions.)
ηὔδα, see αὐδάω.
ἠύτε, *like, as.*
Ἥφαιστος, *Hephaestus,* god of fire; Ἡφαίστοιο, gen. (§ 12).
ἠώς, *dawn.*

θάλασσα, *sea.*
θάνατος, *death;* θανάτοιο, gen. (§ 12).
θάνε, see θνήσκω.
θάπτω, *bury.*
θαρσαλέος, *bold.*
θάρσος, *boldness.*
θαῦμα, *wonder.*
θεά, *goddess.*
θείνω, *strike, slay.*
θεῖος, *of divine origin.*
θέλγω, *charm* (in both good and bad senses).
θεός, *god;* θεοῖο, gen. (§ 12).
Θερσίλοχος, *Thersilochus,* a Trojan.
θέσαν, see τίθημι.
θεσπιδαής, *god-kindled.* (Leaf thinks however that the reference is not so much to the origin of fire as to the fact that fire is stronger than man.)
θῆκεν, see τίθημι.
θήν, *surely* (usually ironical).

θήρ, *wild beast.*
θηρητήρ, *hunter.*
θητεύω, *serve;* θητεύσαμεν, aor.
θνήσκω, *die;* ἔθανε, aor. (θάνε, imper.).
θνητός, *mortal.*
θοός, *swift;* θοῇσιν, dat. pl. fem (§ 12).
θοῦρος, *furious.*
Θρασίος, *Thrasius,* a Trojan.
θρύον, *rush* (plant).
θρώσκω, *leap.*
θυγάτηρ, *daughter;* θυγατέρος, gen. (θυγατρῶν, pl.).
θύελλα, *storm.*
θυμός, *spirit, life, mind.*
θύραζε (= θύρασδε, § 26), lit. *to doors,* i.e. *out.*
θυσσανόεις, *fringed.*
θύω, *rush.*
θωρηκτής, *armed with a breastplate;* θωρηκτῇσιν, dat. pl. (§ 12).

ἴα = μία, fem. of εἷς, *one.*
ἴαχον, aor. or impf. of ἰάχω, *resound.*
Ἴδη, *Ida,* mountain near Troy.
ἱδρώς, *sweat.*
ἴδωμαι, ἰδών, see ὁράω.
ἴει, ἱέμενος, see ἵημι.
ἰέναι, see εἶμι.
ἱερεύω, *sacrifice.*
ἷζον, impf. of ἵζω, *sit.*
ἵημι, *send;* ἵει, pres. imper.; ἧκε, aor.; ἱέμενος, pres. part. mid. (= *desiring*); εἴσομαι, fut. mid. (= *will hasten*).
Ἰήσων, *Jason,* the leader of the Argonauts.
ἰθυπτίων, *straight-flying* (from ἰθύς and πέτομαι).
ἰθύς, see § 23; ἀν' ἰθύν = *upwards along one's aim,* i.e. *straight up* (apparently from a noun ἰθύς).
ἵκανε, impf. of ἱκάνω, *come.*
ἱκέτης, *suppliant;* ἱκέταο, gen. (§ 12).
ἵκω, *come;* ἷξον, aor. (§ 13 *b*);

50   THE ILIAD, TWENTY-FIRST BOOK

ἵκετο and ἵκηται may come from ἵκω or from ἱκόμην, aor. of ἱκνέομαι, *come*.

Ἰλήϊος, *Ileian*, name of a plain near Troy, but only mentioned here.

Ἴλιος, *Ilium*, *Troy*; Ἰλιόφι, see § 26.

ἰλύς, *slime*.

ἱμάς, *strap, thong*.

Ἴμβριος, *Imbrian*. Imbros is an island in the Aegean.

ἴμεν, ἴομεν, see εἶμι.

ἵνα, *in order that*.

ἴξον, see ἵκω.

ἰοχέαιρα, *showerer* (χέω) *of arrows*: epithet of Artemis.

ἱπποκορυστής, *equipped with horses*, or *arrayer of horses* (i.e. chariots).

ἵππος, *horse*.

ἴρηξ, *hawk*.

ἱρός (= ἱερός), *holy, sacred*, or (of cities) perhaps *strong* which possibly was the original meaning of the word.

ἴς, *might*.

ἴσαν, see εἶμι.

ἴσος, *equal to, like*; ἴσα, adv. (§ 20 b).

ἰσοφαρίζω, *vie with* (with dat.).

ἵστημι, *make to stand*; ἵστη, pres. imper. act.; ἵστατο, impf. mid.; στήσεσθαι, fut. mid.; in intrans. sense ἔστη, στήτην, aor. ind.; στῆναι, aor. inf.; ἑστήκει, plup. (with impf. meaning).

ἴσχω, *check*.

ἰτέα, *willow*.

ἶφι, *by force*: adv. from neut. of ἶφις, *mighty* (§ 20 b).

ἰχθύς, *fish*.

ἰών, see εἶμι.

κάγκανος, *dry*.

κάδ = κατά (§ 10 a).

καθίημι, *let down*.

καθύπερθε(ν), *from above, above*.

καί, *and, even, also*.

καίω (= καϝγω?), *burn*; καῖε, impf. and imper.; καίετο, καίοντο, impf. pass.; κῆεν, aor. ind. act. (κῆαι, opt.).

κακός, *bad, evil*, though not necessarily in a moral sense; κακῶς, adv.

κάλλιπες = κατέλιπες, aor. of καταλείπω, *leave* (§ 10 a).

καλός, *fair, seemly, good*; κάλλιστος, superl.

καλύπτω, *cover, place as a covering*; κάλυψε(ν), aor.; κεκάλυπτο, plup. pass.; κεκαλυμμένα, pf. part. pass.

κάματος, *weariness*.

κάμε, aor. of κάμνω, *grow weary*.

καμπύλος, *curved*.

καπνός, *smoke*.

καρπός, (a) *fruit, produce*; (b) *wrist*.

κάρτιστος (= κράτιστος), *strongest*.

καρχαλέος, *rough*.

κασιγνήτη, *sister*; κασίγνητος, *brother*.

κασσίτερος *tin*, possibly alloyed with silver; κασσιτέροιο, gen. (§ 12).

κατά, see § 23.

κατάγω, *lead down*.

κατακτάμεν(αι), inf. of κατέκταν, aor. of κατακτείνω, *slay* (§ 15 b).

κατείβω, *let flow down*.

κατεναντίον, *opposite to*.

κατέσβεσε, aor. of κατασβέννυμι, *quench*.

κατεσθίω, *devour*.

κατέσσυτο, aor. (§ 13 c) of κατασεύομαι, *rush down* (or *back*) *into*.

κάτθανε = κατέθανε, aor. of καταθνήσκω, *die*.

κε(ν), see § 18 (d).

κεῖθεν (= ἐκεῖθεν), *thence*.

κεῖμαι, *lie*; κεῖσο, pres. imper.; κείσεται, fut.; κεῖτο, κεῖντο, impf.

VOCABULARY

κείρω, *shear away.*

κεκαλυμμένα, κεκάλυπτο, see καλύπτω.

κέκλετο, aor. (§ 13 *d*) of κέλομαι, *urge, bid.*

κεκλιμένον, pf. part. pass. of κλίνω, *lean.*

κεκονιμένοι, see κονίζω.

κεκοτηότι, pf. part. (§ 13*f*) of κοτέω, *be angry.*

κελάδεινος, *noisy, shouting.* Epithet of Artemis as a huntress.

κελάδω, *sound, roar.*

κελαινεφής, *dark with clouds, dark.*

κελαρύζω, *murmur.*

κελεύω, *order.*

κεραΐζω, *destroy.*

κεραυνός, originally *thunderbolt,* then *thunder* and *lightning* generally.

κεφαλή, *head.*

κεχόλωτο, see χολόω.

κῆαι, κήεν, see καίω.

κῆδος, *grief.*

κήδω, *vex.*

κῆπος, *garden, orchard.*

κῆρ, (*a*) *heart;* κηρόθι, § 26; (*b*) *fate:* probably originally a winged demon, one of the ghosts of the departed, who carried off souls to Hades (Leaf).

κίε, κίομεν, aor. or impf. of a vb. =*go.*

κιχάνω, *reach, attain, overtake;* κιχείομεν, aor. subj. (§ 15*a*); κιχήσεσθαι, fut. inf. mid.; κιχήσατο, aor. ind. mid.

κληΐς, *collar-bone.*

κλονέω, *drive in confusion;* κλονέοντο, impf. pass.

κλόνος, *confused throng.*

κλυτός, *famous.*

κνήμη, *leg.*

κνημίς, *greave.*

κνημός, *slope* or *shoulder* of a mountain.

κνίση, *savour.*

κοῖλος, *hollow.*

κόλπος, *gulf.*

κοναβέω, *rattle, clang;* κονάβησε, aor.

κοναβίζω, *resound;* κονάβιζεν, impf.

κονίη, *dust.*

κονίζω, *defile with dust;* κεκονιμένοι, pf. part. pass.

κόρυς, *helmet.*

κορύσσω, *equip with a helmet*— hence, applied to a crest of a wave, *arch, uprear.*

κούρη, *maiden;* κοῦρος, *youth.*

κραδίη (=καρδία), *heart.*

κραιπνός, *swift.*

κραταιός, *mighty.*

κρατερός, *strong;* κρατερῆφι, § 26.

κρατέω, *be strong, conquer.*

κρείσσων, *stronger.*

κρείων, *lord, ruler.*

κρημνός, *bank;* κρημνοῖο and κρημνοῦ, gen. (§ 12).

κρήνη, *spring.*

Κρόνος, *Cronus,* father of Zeus.

Κρονίδης, Κρονίων, *son of Cronus,* i.e. Zeus.

κρύπτω, *hide.*

κτείνω, *slay;* κτάνε, aor. ind.; κτεῖναι, aor. inf.

κυβίστων, impf. of κυβιστάω, *plunge.*

κυδιάω, *exult;* κυδιόωντες, pres. part. (§ 10*i*).

κῦδος, *fame.*

κυκάω, *stir.*

κυλλοπόδιον, probably a pe form of κύλλοπος, *little crook foot* (Leaf). Epithet of He phaestus.

κῦμα, *wave.*

κυνάμυια, *dog-fly,* i.e. *shameles one*—as shameless as a dog and as bold as a fly (Leaf).

κύπειρον, *sedge.*

κύψας, aor. part. of κύπτω, *stoop.*

κύων, *dog, bitch;* κύον, voc.

51

4—2

λᾶας, *stone.*
λάβε, λάβῃσιν, λαβών, see λαμ-βάνω.
λάβρος, *furious.*
λαιψηρός, *nimble, swift.*
λαμβάνω, *seize, take;* λάβε, aor. ind. (λαβών, part.; λάβῃσιν, 3rd sing. subj., § 14).
Λαοθόη, *Laothoe,* mother of Lycaon.
Λαομέδων, *Laomedon,* a former king of Troy.
λαός, *people, soldiers.*
λέβης, *caldron.*
λείπω, *leave;* λεῖπεν, impf.; λίπεν, aor.
Λέλεγες, *Leleges*—a tribe in the Troad; Λελέγεσσι, dat. pl. (§ 12).
λευγαλέος, *lamentable, sorry.*
λευκώλενος, *white-armed.*
λέχος, *couch;* λεχέεσσι, dat. pl. (§ 12).
λέων, *lion.*
λήγω, *cease.*
Λῆμνος, *Lemnos,* island in Aegean; Λήμνοιο, gen. (§ 12).
Λητώ, *Leto,* mother of Apollo and Artemis; Λητοῖ, voc.; Λητώ, acc.
λιασθείς, aor. part. of λιάζομαι, *withdraw.*
λίην, *overmuch, excessively.*
λίθος, *stone.*
λιλαίομαι, *desire.*
λιμήν, *haven.*
λίμνη, *pool, mere, sea.*
λίπε(ν), see λείπω.
λοεσσάμενος, aor. part. mid. of λοέω, *wash* (§ 8).
λοίγιος, *destructive, deadly.*
λοιγός, *destruction, death.*
Λυκάων, *Lycaon,* son of Priam.
λύσσα, *fury, frenzy.*
λύω, *loose;* in middle *ransom;* λῦσε, aor. act.; λύμην, λύτο, aor. pass. (§ 13 c).
λωτός, perhaps a kind of clover.
λωφάω, *abate.*

μαίνομαι, *rage;* μαίνετο, impf.
μάκελλα, *pick-axe* (with one point).
μακρός, *long,* in 197 *deep.*
μάλα, *very, greatly, assuredly;* μᾶλλον, compar.
μαλερός, *mighty.*
μάρπτω, *grasp, overtake.*
μάχη, *battle.*
μάχομαι, *fight* (with dat.); μαχήσομαι, fut.; μαχοίατο, 3rd pl. pres. opt. (§ 14).
μαψιδίως, *thoughtlessly.*
με, see ἐγώ.
μεγάθυμος, *high-minded, great-hearted.*
μεγακήτης, *with mighty maw:* a rather doubtful word, applied here to a dolphin, elsewhere to the sea and ships (Leaf).
μεγαλήτωρ, *great-hearted.*
μέγαρον, *hall, house.*
μέγας, *great;* μεγάλοιο, gen. sing. (§ 12); μεγάλῃσιν, dat. pl. fem. (§ 12).
μεθίημι, *let loose, throw* (with acc.), *cease from* (with gen.); μεθίει, impf.; μεθῆκε, aor.
μειδάω, μειδιάω, *smile;* μείδησεν, aor.; μειδιόωσα, pres. part. fem. (§ 10 i).
μείλινος, *ashen.*
μειλίχιος, *soft, soothing.*
μελάνυδρος, *with dark water.*
μέλας, *black, gloomy.*
μέλδω, *melt.*
μέλεος, *wretched, sorry;* μέλεον, advb. = *'for nothing'* (Leaf).
μελίη, *ash, spear of ash-wood.*
μέλλω, *intend, be about to, be likely to.*
μέμαα, μέμονα, pf. of μάω (?), *desire, be minded.*
μέμβλετο (= μέμελετο), aor. mid. of μέλω, *be a care* (Leaf), cf. § 13 d.
μέμνῃ, μέμνηαι, 2nd sing. (§ 14) of μέμνημαι (= *remember*), pf. mid. of μιμνήσκω, *remind.*

μεμυκώς, pf. part. of μυκάω, *bellow*.

μέν, *emphatic particle, usually untranslateable*. In Homer μέν...δέ often *imply little or no contrast* (Leaf).

μενεαίνω, *desire*.

Μενοιτιάδης, *son of Menoetius;* Μενοιτιάδαο, gen. (§ 12).

μένος, *might*.

μένω, *remain;* μενέουσιν, fut.

μέρμερος, *baneful*.

μέσος, *middle;* μέσσῳ, dat. (§ 8).

μεσσοπαγής, *up to the middle*.

μετά, see § 23.

μεταῖξας, aor. of μεταίσσω, *rush after*.

μέτελθε, aor. imper. of μετέρχομαι, *follow, pursue*.

μετέσσυτο, aor. (§ 13 c) of μετασεύομαι, *rush after*.

μευ, see ἐγώ.

μή, *not, lest*.

μηδέ, *neither, nor, not even*.

μήδομαι, *plan;* μήδετο, impf.

μῆνις, *wrath*.

μηρός, *thigh*.

μήτε, *neither, nor*.

μήτηρ, *mother*.

μιαιφόνος, *bloodstained*.

μίγη, aor. pass. (μιγήμεναι, inf. § 15 b) of μίγνυμι, *mix with, contend with, wed*.

μίν, *him, her, it*.

μινυνθάδιος, *short-lived*.

μισθός, *pay;* μισθοῖο and μισθοῦ, gen. (§ 12).

Μνῆσος, *Mnesus*, a Trojan.

μόγις, *with difficulty*.

μόθος, *battle*.

μοι, see ἐγώ.

μοῖρα, *fate*.

μορμύρων, *boiling*.

μόρος, *fate*.

μοῦνος, *alone* (§ 10 d).

Μύδων, *Mydon*, a Trojan.

μυθέομαι, *say, speak*.

μῦθος, *speech, word*.

μυρίκη, *tamarisk;* μυρίκῃσιν, dat. pl. (§ 12).

μυρίος, *countless*.

Μυρμιδών, *Myrmidon*, follower of Achilles; Μυρμιδόνεσσιν, dat. pl. (§ 12).

μυχός, *recess*.

μώνυξ, *with solid hoofs.* (Leaf says it is not connected with μόνος, but = σμώνυξ. The first syllable seems to be connected with μία (i.e. σμία, cf. Latin *sim-plex*).)

νάω, *flow*.

νεβρός, *fawn*.

νεικέω, *revile;* νείκεσε, aor. (§ 10 c).

νεῖκος, *strife*.

νειόθι, *at the bottom* (§ 26).

νεκρός, *corpse*.

νέκυς, *corpse;* νεκύεσσι, dat. pl. (§ 12).

νεοαρδής, *freshly-watered*.

νέομαι, *go, return* (often in a future sense).

νέος, *new, young, fresh*.

νεότευκτος, *newly-wrought*.

νευρά, *bowstring;* νευρῆφιν § 26.

νεφεληγερέτα, *cloud-gathering* (§ 12); νεφεληγερέταο, gen. (§ 12).

νηλεής, *pitiless*.

νήπιος, νηπύτιος, *childish, foolish*.

νῆσος, *island*.

νηῦς, *ship;* νῆας, acc. pl.; νηυσίν, dat. pl.

νικάω, *conquer*.

νίκη, *victory*.

νοέω, *perceive*.

νόσφιν, see § 23.

Νότος, *south-wind;* Νότοιο, gen. (§ 12).

νύ, νῦν, see § 5.

νῶϊ, see ἐγώ.

νῶτον, *back*.

Ξάνθος, *Xanthus,* river near Troy, also called Scamander; **Ξανθοῖο,** gen. (§ 12).

ξεῖνος, *friend, stranger.*

ξίφος, *sword.*

ξύλον, *wood.*

ξύλοχος, *thicket;* ξυλόχοιο, gen. (§ 12).

ξυμβλήμεναι, aor. inf. (§ 13 *c,* 15 *b*), of **ξυμβάλλω,** *engage* (in battle).

ξυνελαύνω, *bring into conflict.*

ξυνίοντας, part. of **ξύνειμι,** *contend.*

ὁ, see § 16; **ταί,** nom. pl. fem.; **τοῖο,** gen. (§ 12).

ὅδε, *this.*

ὄζος, *shoot:*

οἱ, (*a*) nom. pl. of **ὁ**; (*b*) dat. of **ἑ.**

οἵ, see **ὅς.**

οἶδα, *know* (but often in Homer denotes disposition or character rather than mere knowledge); **εἰδῇς,** subj.; **εἴσεαι,** fut. ind. (§ 14).

οἶδμα, *swell, wave.*

οἶμα, *swoop.*

οἰμώζω, *groan, lament;* ᾤμωξεν, aor. (**οἰμώξας,** part.).

οἶος, *alone.*

οἷος, *what kind of man;* **οἷον δή,** *even as now* (Leaf), cf. § 20 *b.*

οἴσει, see **φέρω.**

ὀιστός, *arrow.*

ὀίω, *think.*

ὀλέεσθαι, fut. inf. mid.; **ὀλέεσθε,** fut. ind. mid.; **ὀλέσσαι,** aor. inf. act. (§ 8) of **ὄλλυμι,** *destroy.*

ὄλεκεν, impf. of **ὀλέκω,** *ruin, destroy.*

ὀλοός, *baneful.*

ὀλοφύρομαι, *lament;* ὀλοφύρεαι, 2nd sing. (§ 14).

Ὄλυμπος, Οὔλυμπος, *Olympus,* mountain in North Greece; supposed to be home of the gods; **Οὔλυμπόνδε** § 26.

ὅμιλος, *throng.*

ὁμογάστριος, *full brother.*

ὁμοῖος, *common to all.*

ὀμοῦμαι, fut. of **ὄμνυμι,** *swear.*

ὀμφαλός, *navel.*

ὁμῶς, *in like manner.*

ὀνείδειος, *taunting.*

ὀνομάζω, *name, address;* **ὀνόμαζεν,** impf.

ὀξύς, *sharp.*

ὄπα, acc. of **ὄψ,** *voice.*

ὀπάζω, *make to accompany,* hence *give.*

ὄπιθεν, ὄπισθε, ὀπίσσω, *behind* (§ 8).

ὁπότε, ὁππότε, *when* (§ 8).

ὀπωρινός, *autumnal.*

ὅπως, *how, in order that.*

ὁράω, *see;* **ὁράᾳς,** 2nd sing. pres. ind. (§ 10 *i*); **ὁρᾶτο,** impf. mid.; **εἶδον,** aor. (**ἰδών,** part.; **ἴδωμαι,** subj. mid.).

ὀρίνω, *stir, excite;* **ὄρινε,** impf.

ὁρμάω, *hurry, be eager;* **ὡρμᾶτο,** impf. mid.; **ὁρμήσειε,** aor. opt. act.; **ὡρμήσατο,** aor. ind. mid.

ὄρνυμι, *stir, rouse;* in middle *rush;* **ὤρνυτο,** impf. mid.; **ὄρσουσα,** fut. part. act.; **ὦρτο,** aor. ind. mid. (**ὄρμενον,** part.); **ὄρσεο,** aor. imper. mid. (§ 13 *b, c*).

ὀρόθυνον, aor. imper. of **ὀροθύνω,** *stir up.*

ὀρούω, *rush.*

ὄρπηξ, *shoot* (of plants).

ὀρυμαγδός, *din.*

ὄρχαμος, *leader.*

ὅς, (*a*) relative, *who, which* (§ 16); **τοί,** nom. pl.; (*b*) personal, *he* (§ 16); (*c*) possessive, *his, her.* For **ὅ, ὅτι,** etc., see note on 150.

ὅσος, ὄσσος, *as much* (*many*) *as* (§ 8).

ὁσσάκι, *as often as.*

ὄσσε (dual), *eyes.*

ὀστέον, *bone.*

ὅστις, *who.*

ὅτε, *when, since.*
ὅτι, see ὅς.
ὀτρύνω, *urge;* ὀτρυνέων, fut. (or pres.) part.
οὐ, οὐκ, οὐχ, *not.*
οὔατα, pl. of οὖς, *ear.*
οὐδέ, *neither, nor, not even.*
οὐκέτι, *no longer.*
οὖλος, *baneful.*
οὖν, see § 5.
οὕνεκα, *because.*
Οὐρανίωνες, *heavenly ones, gods.*
οὐρανός, *heaven*—the brazen firmament in which the stars were fixed (Bayfield); οὐρανόθεν, § 26.
οὔρεα, pl. of ὄρος, *mountain.*
οὖρος, *boundary.*
οὐτάω, *wound;* οὐτάμεναι, pres. inf. (§ 15 *b*); οὔτησε, aor. ind. ; οὐτάσῃ, aor. subj. (from οὐτάζω).
οὔτε, *neither, nor.*
οὕτως, *thus.*
ὄφελε, aor. of ὀφείλω, *owe;* ὡς ὤφελε = *would that.*
'Οφελέστης, *Ophelestes,* a Trojan.
ὀφθαλμός, *eye.*
ὄφρα, *in order that.*
ὀχετηγός, *constructing a channel.*
ὀχεύς, *bar, bolt;* ὀχῆας, acc. pl.
ὀχθέω, *be vexed.*
ὄχθη, *bank.*
ὀχλεῦνται, 3rd pl. pres. ind. pass. (§ 10 *g*) of ὀχλέω, *move.*
ὀψέ, *late.*

πάθομεν, aor. (πάθοιμι, opt., παθών, part.) of πάσχω, *suffer.*
Παίονες, *Paeonians,* living both in Troad and in Macedonia.
Παιονίη, *Paeonia.*
παῖς, *son.*
πάλαι, *of old, long ago.*
παλάμη, *hand;* παλάμῃσιν, dat. pl. (§ 12).
πάλιν, *again, back.*

Παλλάς, *Pallas,* another name of Athena.
πάμπαν, *altogether, at all.*
παμφανόων, *bright-shining.*
πανόψιος, *visible to all.*
πάντοθεν, *from every side.*
πάντοσε, *in all directions.*
πάρ (§ 10 *a*), παρά, see § 23 ; πάρα = πάρεστι, *is present.*
παράκοιτις, *wife.*
πάρδαλις, *panther.*
παρεστάμεναι, *stand by, help,* pf. inf. (intrans.) of παρίστημι (§ 15 *b*).
πᾶς, *all.*
πασάμην, aor. of πατέομαι, *eat.*
πάταγος, *din.*
πατήρ, *father.*
πατροκασίγνητος, *father's brother;* πατροκασιγνήτοιο, gen. (§ 12).
Πάτροκλος, *Patroclus,* friend of Achilles, slain by Hector.
πατρώιος, *belonging to a father.*
παύω, *stop;* παύσομεν, aor. subj. (§ 15 *a*); παυσάσθην, aor. mid. dual; παυσώμεσθα, aor. subj. mid.
παχύς, *thick, stout.*
πεδίον, *plain;* πεδίοιο, gen.; πεδίονδε, § 26.
πειράομαι, *try, try conclusions with;* πειρᾷ, 2nd sing. pres. ; πειρήσαιτο (§ 10 *h*), aor. opt. ; πειρηθῆναι, aor. inf.
πέλεθρον, *rood:* probably originally a measure of length (perhaps of furrow = *furlong*), then of area.
πέλεια, *dove.*
πελέμιξεν, aor. of πελεμίζω, *shake.*
πελώριος, *prodigious* (Leaf).
πέμπω, *send;* πέμψεν, aor.
πεπαρμένη, pf. part. pass. of πείρω, *pierce.*
πεπερημένος, see περάω.
πεπταμένας, see πετάννυμι.
πεπτ(ε)ῶτα, see πίπτω.

περ, see § 5.
περάω,(a) export and sell; περάαν,
fut. inf. (§ 10 i); ἐπέρασσα,
aor. (§ 8); πεπερημένος, pf.
part. pass. (§ 10 h); (b) cross,
pierce; ἐπέρησε, aor.; περῶντα,
pres. part.
περί, see § 23.
Περίβοια, Periboea.
περιδδείσασα, aor. part. of περι-
δείδω, fear greatly (§ 8).
περιδέξιος, ambidextrous.
περιχεύας, aor. part. of περιχέω
(= χέρω), pour around.
πέρσειαν, aor. opt. ; πέρσειν,
fut. inf. of πέρθω, sack.
πέσε, πεσών, see πίπτω.
πετάννυμι, spread; πετάσσας,
aor. part. (§ 8); πετασθεῖσαι,
aor. part. pass.; πεπταμένας,
pf. part. pass. (= open).
πετεηνός, winged, bird.
πέτομαι, fly.
πέτρη, rock (§ 10 h).
πεφεύγοι, see φεύγω.
πεφιδέσθαι, aor. inf. (§ 13 d) of
φείδομαι, spare (with gen.).
πεφοβήατο, see φοβέω.
πεφυζότες, in flight, see note on 6.
πεφύκει, see φύω.
πη, in any way.
πηγή, spring.
Πήδασος, Pedasus, a town in the
Troad.
πηδάω, leap.
Πηλεγών, Pelegon, a Trojan.
Πηλείδης, Πηλείων, child of
Peleus, i.e. Achilles; Πηλείδαο, gen. (§ 12).
Πηλεύς, Peleus; Πηλέος, gen.
Πηλιάς, adjective of Πήλιον,
Pelion, a mountain range in
Thessaly.
πῆχυς, fore-arm.
πίθηαι, 2nd sing. aor. subj.
(§ 14) of πείθομαι, be per-
suaded.
πί(μ)πλημι, fill; πλῆτο, aor.
pass. (§ 13 c).

πίπτω, fall; ἔπεσον, πέσε, aor.;
πεπτ(ε)ῶτα, pf. part. (§ 13 f).
πίτνα, impf. of πίτνημι, spread.
πιφαύσκω, make manifest (by
speech or sight); πιφαύσκεο,
2nd sing. pres. imper. mid.
πλάζ', an impf. or aor. of doubtful
meaning : perhaps connected
with πελάζω (= reached), or
with πλήσσω (= struck).
πλείων, πλέων, compar. of πολύς,
much.
πλῆθ', πλῆτο, see πίμπλημι.
πλήθω, be full.
πληκτίζομαι, bandy blows with,
fight (with dat.).
πλώω, sail; πλῶον, impf.
πνοιή, blast.
ποδάρκης, swift-footed.
πόθεν, whence?
ποινή, atonement.
πολέας, see πολύς.
πολεμίζω, fight.
πολεμιστής, warrior.
πόλεμος, war; πολέμοιο, gen.
(§ 12).
πολιός, grey.
πόλις, city; πόληος, πόλιος,
gen.
πολυγηθής, joyous.
Πολύδωρος, Polydorus, son of
Priam.
πολύμητις, of many wiles.
πολύπτυχος, with many valleys.
πολύς, much, many; πολλόν,
acc.; πολέες, nom. pl.; πολέας,
acc. pl.
πολύφρων, clever.
πόνος, labour; πόνοιο, gen.(§ 12).
πόντος, sea.
πόποι, an exclamation.
πόρος, ford.
πόρφυρε, impf. of πορφύρω,
grow dark (with a swell), hence
perhaps = be troubled or ponder.
πορφύρεος, the dark colour of
disturbed waves (Leaf).
πορών, aor. part. of πόρω (?),
bring to pass.

Ποσειδάων, *Poseidon*, god of the sea.

ποταμός, *river;* ποταμοῖο and ποταμοῦ, gen. (§ 12); ποταμόνδε § 26.

ποτέ, *once, ever.*

ποτί, see πρός.

πότμος, *fate.*

πότνια, *lady, mistress.*

πού, *in some degree, I ween, somewhere.*

πουλυβότειρα, *fertile.*

πούς, *foot;* ποδοῖιν, dual; ποσί, ποσσίν, πόδεσσιν, dat. pl. (§ 12).

πρεσβύτατος, *oldest.*

πρηνής, *headlong.*

Πρίαμος, *Priam*, king of Troy; Πριάμοιοι, gen. (§ 12).

πρίν, *before.*

προαλής, *sloping.*

προμολών, aor. part. of προβλώσκω, *advance.*

προπάροιθε(ν), see § 23.

προρέω, *flow forward.*

πρός, see § 23.

προσέειπε, aor. of προσλέγω, *address* (§ 13 *d*).

προσηύδα, impf. of προσαυδάω, *address.*

πρόσθε, see § 23.

προσφωνέω, *address.*

πρότερος, *former, first* (i.e. before another).

προτί, see πρός.

πρόφρασσα, fem. of πρόφρων, *kindly* or *thoughtful.*

προχέω, *pour forth;* προχέοντο, impf. mid.

πρόχνυ, *utterly* (Leaf).

πρυλέεσσι, dat. (§ 12) of πρυλέες, which is thought to mean either *infantry* or *champions* (Leaf).

πρῶτος, *first;* πρῶτα, adv.

πτελέη, *elm.*

πτερόεις, *fluttering* (Leaf).

πτολεμίζω, see πολεμίζω (§ 8).

πτόλεμος, see πόλεμος, πτολέμοιο, gen. (§ 12).

πτολίεθρον, *city.*

πτολίπορθος, *sacker of cities.*

πτώσσω, *cower;* πτῶσσον, impf.

πυκινός, *dense, numerous;* πυκινῶς, adv. = *closely, strongly, often.*

πυλαωρός, *warder.*

πύλη, *gate.*

πῦρ, *fire.*

πύργος, *fortification, tower.*

πυροφόρος, *wheat-bearing;* πυροφόροιο, gen. (§ 12).

πώ, *yet.*

πῶς, *how?*

ῥά, see ἄρα.

ῥέεθρον, *stream.*

ῥέζω, *do;* ἔρεξε, aor.

ῥέω, *flow;* ῥέε, impf.

ῥῆξε, aor. of ῥήγνυμι, *break.*

ῥητός, *stated, fixed.*

ῥίζη, *root;* ῥιζέων, gen. pl.

ῥινοτόρος, *shield-piercing.*

ῥιπή, *force.*

ῥόος, *stream, channel;* ῥόοιο, gen. (§ 12).

ῥωπήια, *bushes.*

σάκος, *shield.*

σαλπίζω, *sound* (a trumpet); σάλπιγξεν, aor.

σάνις, *board.* In 535 σανίδας perhaps = *door* or boards fastened on it for extra security (Leaf).

σαόφρων, *prudent.*

σαόω (or σάωμι), *save;* σάω, 3rd sing. impf.; σαῶσαι, aor. inf.; σαώσαι, aor. opt.

Σατνιόεις, *Satnioeis*, a river in the Troad.

σέ, σέθεν, σέο, σεῦ, see σύ.

σῆμα, *tomb, barrow.*

σημαίνω, *signify, order.*

σθένος, *might.*

σίαλος, *hog;* σιάλοιο, gen. (§ 12).

Σιμόεις, *Simois*, river near Troy.

σκαιός, *left:* in fem. *left hand.*

Σκάμανδρος, *Scamander*, river near Troy, also called Xanthus.

σκιάζω, *overshadow*.

σκότος, *darkness*.

σμαραγέω, *crash, flash*.

σμερδαλέος, *terrible*.

σοί, see σύ.

σός, *thy*; σῇσιν, τεῇσ', dat. pl. fem. (§ 12).

στείνω, *crowd*.

στενάχω, *groan*.

στεῦτο, impf. or aor. of στεῦμαι (?), *declare*.

στῆθος, *chest*; στήθεσσιν, dat. pl. (§ 12).

στῆναι, στήσεσθαι, στήτην, see ἵστημι.

στηρίζω, *fix*.

στόνος, *groaning*.

στρεπτός, *pliant*(?). In 31 the shirt may be pleated like a kilt, or woven with a diagonal twill (Bayfield), or pleated on shoulder as a pad against weight of corslet (Leaf), or made of twisted strips of leather (Sidgwick).

στροφάλιγξ, *eddy*.

στυφελίζω, *strike fiercely*; στυφέλιξε, aor.

σύ, *thou*; σέ, acc.; σέο, σεῦ, σέθεν (§ 26), gen.; σοί, τοί, dat.; ὑμεῖς, nom. pl.; ὑμῖν, dat. pl.

σύν, see § 23.

συναίνυμαι, *gather*; συναίνυτο, impf.

συνήντετο, impf. of συνάντομαι, *meet* (dat.).

σύτο, aor. mid. (§ 13 c) of σεύομαι, *rush*.

συφορβός, *swineherd*.

σφεδανόν, *eagerly*: perhaps connected with σφόδρα (Leaf).

σφίν, see ἑ.

σχεδόν, *near, almost*.

σχεῖν, σχέτο, σχῶμεν, see ἔχω.

ταθείς, aor. part. pass. of τείνω, *stretch*.

ταί, see ὁ.

τάμνω, *cut*; τάμνε, impf.

ταρβέω, *fear*.

ταῦρος, *bull*.

τάχα, *quickly, soon*; τάχιστα, superl.

ταχύς, *swift*; ταχέεσσι, dat. pl. (§ 12).

τέ, see § 5.

τεῇσ', see σός.

τεθηπώς, part. of pf. τέθηπα (no pres.), *be astonished*.

τείρω, *trouble*; τεῖρε, impf.; τείροντ', impf. pass.

τεῖχος, *wall*.

τέκε, τέκετο, see τίκτω.

τέκνον, τέκος, *child*.

τελέθω, *come into being, be*.

τέλος, *fulfilment*.

τέρπω, *delight*.

τέτρατος, *fourth*.

τεῦχος, *armour*.

τεύχω, *make*: in pass. nearly = *be*; τεῦξαν, aor.; τετεύξεται, fut. pf. pass.; τέτυκται, pf. pass.

τηλεδαπός, *distant*.

τηλόθι, *afar* (§ 26).

τῇ, τῇπερ, *by that way, there, where*.

τίη (perhaps τί ἦ), *why?* (§ 20 b).

τίθημι, *place*; ἔθηκε, θῆκεν, θέσαν, aor.

τίκτω, *beget*; τίκτε, impf.; τέκε, aor. (τέκετο, mid.).

τίνω, *pay for*; τίσετε, aor. subj. (§ 15 a).

τίπτε (= τί ποτε), *why?* (§ 20 b).

τις, *some, any*; τι, *at all* (§ 20 b).

τίς, *who?* τί, *why?* (§ 20 b).

τιτύσκομαι, *prepare* (with acc.), *aim at* (with gen.); τιτύσκετο, impf.

τλήμων, *enduring*, hence *patient, bold, wretched*.

τοί, (a) = σοί, see σύ; (b) = οἵ, see ὅς; (c) particle, see § 5.

τοῖο, see ὁ.

τοῖος, τοιόσδε, τοιοῦτος, *such*.

τοκεύς, *parent*.

τόξον, *bow;* τόξα, *bow and arrows.*

τοξοφόρος, *bow-bearing.*

τόσος, τόσσος, *so great, so much* (§ 8).

τοσσάκι, *so often* (§ 8).

τότε, *then.*

τόφρα, *so long, then.*

τρέμω, *tremble;* τρέμε, impf.

τρέπω, *turn;* τρέπεν, impf. ; τρέψε, aor.; ἐτράπετο, aor. mid.

τρέω, *shrink.*

τρηχύς, *rough.*

τρίς, *thrice.*

Τροίη, *Troy.*

Τρωικός, Τρώς, *Trojan;* Τρωσί, Τρώεσσι, dat. pl. (§ 12).

τρωτός, *vulnerable.*

Τυδείδης, *son of Tydeus,* i.e. Diomedes.

τυμβοχοῆσαι, aor. inf. of τυμβοχοέω, *raise a barrow.*

τύπτω, *strike;* τύπτε, impf.; τύψε, aor.

τυτθός, *little.*

τῴ, *in that case.* See note on 190.

ὕδωρ, *water.*

υἱός, *son;* υἱεῖ and υἱέι, dat.; υἷές, nom. pl.

ὑλαγμός, *barking.*

ὑλήεις, *woody.*

ὕπαιθα, see § 23.

ὑπαίσσω, *dart beneath* (or *up to*).

ὑπέδραμε, aor. of ὑποτρέχω, *run in under.*

ὑπεκπροθέων, *running on before* (§ 24).

ὑπεκπροφεύγω, *run away secretly* (§ 24).

ὑπέρ, see § 23.

ὑπερέπτω, *eat away from beneath;* ὑπέρεπτε, impf.

ὕπερθεν, *from above, above.*

ὑπέρμορον (possibly two words), *beyond what is fated.*

ὑπερφίαλος, *proud, puissant.*

ὑπέστη, aor. (ὑποστάς, part.) of ὑφίστημι, *undertake.*

ὑπό, see § 23.

ὑποθησόμεθα, fut. mid. of ὑποτίθημι, *suggest.*

ὑποκλονέομαι, *be driven in confusion.*

ὑσμίνη, *combat.*

ὑψηλός, *high;* ὑψηλοῖο, gen. (§ 12).

ὑψίπυλος, *high-gated.*

ὑψόσε, *on high.*

φάγῃσι, see ἐσθίω.

φαεινός, *bright.*

φαίδιμος, *glorious.*

φάος, *light,* (metaph.) *joy.*

φάσγανον, *sword.*

φάσιν, φάτο, see φημί.

φέρτερος, *stronger, braver.*

φέρω, *bear;* οἴσει, fut.·

φεύγω, *flee;* φεῦγ᾽ impf.; φευγέμεναι, pres. inf. (§ 15 *b*); φύγῃσι, φύγῃ, aor. subj. (§ 14); πεφεύγοι, pf. opt.; φεύξεσθαι, fut. inf.

φηγός, *oak.*

φημί, *say;* φάσιν, 3rd pl. pres.; φῆσθα, 2nd sing. impf.; ἔφη, φῆ, aor. act.; ἔφαθ᾽, φάτο, aor. mid.

φθάνω, *outstrip;* φθάμενος, aor. part. mid.

φθέγγομαι, *speak;* φθέγξατο, aor.; φθέγξομαι, aor. subj. (§ 15 *a*).

φθείρω, *destroy.*

φθινύθω, *waste away.*

φιλοπτόλεμος, *war-loving.*

φίλος, *friend, friendly, own* (perhaps the original sense); φίλτερος, compar.

φιτρός, *log.*

φλεγέθω, *blaze.*

φλέγμα, *flame, fire.*

φλέγω, *burn* (trans. and intrans.); φλέγετο, impf. mid.

φλόξ, *flame.*

φλύω, *boil.*

φοβέω, *frighten;* φοβέοντο, impf. pass.; πεφοβήατο, 3rd pl. plup. pass. (§ 14).

Φοῖβος, *Phoebus*, name of Apollo.
φόνος, *death, slaughter.*
φορέω, *bring, bear, wear;* φορέεσκον, past (§ 13 *a*).
φρεῖαρ, *well;* φρείατα, pl.
φρήν, *heart, mind;* φρεσί, dat. pl.
φρίξ, *ripple.*
φύγῃ, φύγῃσι, see φεύγω.
φύλλον, *leaf.*
φυσίζοος, *life-giving.*
φυτόν, *plant.*
φύω, *make to grow;* πεφύκει, plup. (intrans.).
φωνέω, *speak.*
φώς, *man.*

χαίρω, *rejoice;* χαῖρε, impf.
χαίτη, *hair.*
χαλεπός, *terrible, hard.*
χάλκεος, *made of bronze.*
χαλκοβατής, *with floor of bronze.*
χαλκός seems to denote *bronze*, or *copper* or *metal* generally.
χαμᾶζε, *to the ground.*
χαμαί, *on the ground.*
χάρις, *gratitude, favour.*
χειμών, *storm, winter.*
χείρ, *hand;* χερσίν, dat. pl.
χέραδος, *silt.*
χέρσονδε, *to the land* (§ 26).
χηραμός, *hole.*
χθών, *ground, earth.*
χιτών, *tunic.*
χολάδες, *bowels.*
χολόω, *provoke to anger;* χολώσατο, aor. mid.

χραισμέω, *help;* χραισμησέμεν, fut. inf. (§ 15 *b*).
χρέω, *need* (noun).
χρυσός, *gold.*
χρώς, *skin, flesh;* χροός, gen.
χύντο, aor. mid. of χέω (=χεϝω), *pour* (§ 13 *c*).
χώομαι, *be angry;* χώετο, impf.
χῶρος, *place.*

ψάμαθος, *sand.*
ψεύδης, *false;* ψεύδεσσιν, dat. pl.
ψηφίς, *pebble.*
ψυχή, *life.*

ὤ, *exclamation.*
ὧδε, *thus, so.*
ὠθέω, *thrust;* ὦθει, impf.; ὦσε, aor.
'Ωκεανός, *Oceanus*, the river thought to flow round the earth; 'Ωκεανοῖο, gen. (§ 12).
ὠκύς, *swift;* ὤκιστος, superl.; ὦκα, adv.
ὦμος, *shoulder.*
ὤμωξεν, see οἰμώζω.
ὦνος, *price.*
Ὧραι, *hours, seasons* (personified).
ὤρμαινε, impf.; ὤρμηνεν, aor. of ὁρμαίνω, *ponder.*
ὤρνυτο, ὦρτο, see ὄρνυμι.
ὡς, (*a*) *as, when:* (*b*) *in order that;* (*c*) in exclamatory sense, see notes on 273 and 279.
ὥς, *thus, so.*
ὤσας, ὦσε, see ὠθέω.
ὡσεί, *as if.*
ὠτειλή, *wound.*

For EU product safety concerns, contact us at Calle de José Abascal, 56–1°,
28003 Madrid, Spain or eugpsr@cambridge.org.

www.ingramcontent.com/pod-product-compliance
Ingram Content Group UK Ltd.
Pitfield, Milton Keynes, MK11 3LW, UK
UKHW020312140625
459647UK00018B/1843